Robert H. Reardon

EDUCATING
FOR
SERVICE

EDUCATING FOR SERVICE

ESSAYS PRESENTED TO
Robert H. Reardon

Edited by James Earl Massey

WARNER PRESS
ANDERSON, INDIANA

Dedicatory Letter
to
Robert H. Reardon

Dear Dr. Reardon:

The scholar-churchmen and friends whose writings appear in this volume in your honor join with a far larger host of persons in commending your life and services as you retire from your twenty-five-year presidency at Anderson College.

Your life and labors have personified the close ties that exist between life and learning, study and service, wisdom and work, the Church and the Academy. You belong to the company of the Doctors of the Church. Your high scholarship combined with a devout faith and an unfailing commitment to service have long since marked you as an exemplary figure among us. Few persons among us have been so well suited to the responsibilities you have carried for so many years, and fewer still could have gained and held the admiration and cooperation of both the Church and the campus community as you have done during your tenure as president. This volume is one of the many tributes your life has merited, and we are most grateful that your services gave us occasion to share our commendation in this way.

As you enter upon a new phase of your life, be assured that you have left a lasting legacy; but be assured, as well, that you carry with you our trust, unfailing appreciation, prayers, and love.

In abiding friendship,

James Earl Massey
Editor

Robert H. Reardon

Curriculum Vitae

Born: April 27, 1919, at Chicago, Illinois, to Dr. E. A. Reardon and his wife, Pearl.

Education: Bachelor of Arts, Anderson College; Bachelor of Divinity, Oberlin Graduate School of Theology; Master of Sacred Theology, Oberlin Graduate School of Theology; Doctor of Ministry, Vanderbilt University; Graduate Study, University of Michigan and Harvard University; Doctor of Humane Letters, DePauw University; Doctor of Laws, Anderson College.

Posts Held: Pastorates at Loudonville, Ohio; Kipton, Ohio; and Chester, Pennsylvania, 1943-1947; Assistant to the President and Instructor in Religion, Anderson College, 1947-1952; Executive Vice-President, Anderson College, 1952-1958; President, Anderson College, 1958-1983; President Emeritus, 1983—.

Memberships: Indiana State Scholarship Commission; Commission on Higher Education of the National Council of Churches; Anderson-Madison County Hospital Development Program, cochairperson; St. John's Hickey Memorial Hospital, Advisory Board; Anderson YMCA, Board of Directors; Community Hospital, Anderson, Advisory Board; Anderson Chamber of Commerce, Board of Directors; Madison County Chapter of American Red Cross, Board of Directors; Wilson's Boys Club of Anderson, Board of Directors; Anderson Council of Social Agencies, President; State of Indiana Constitutional Revision Commission; United Way of Madison County, Past General

Campaign Chairperson; Anderson Community Schools Blue Ribbon Committee (1978), Chairperson; St. John's Medical Center Building and Health Planning Committees; Indiana Conference on Higher Education, Past President; The Independent Colleges and Universities of Indiana, Past President; Associated Colleges of Indiana, Past President; Executive Council of the Church of God, Anderson, Indiana; Anderson Kiwanis Club; International Platform Association.

Honors and Recognitions: Sagamore of the Wabash Award; Toner Award for Contributions to International Understanding; Liberty Bell Award; Anderson College Distinguished Service Award; *Who's Who in America; Who's Who in Education; Who's Who in the Midwest; Who's Who in American College and University Administration; Men of Achievement; Who's Who in Religion; Outstanding Educators of America; Community Leaders and Noteworthy Americans; Contemporary Notables; International Who's Who in Community Service; Who's Who in the United States; Dictionary of International Biography;* Distinguished American Educator Award for Eisenhower Memorial Scholarship Foundation; 1982 Anderson Lions Club "Man of the Year" Award.

Writings: The Early Morning Light (Anderson, Ind.: Warner Press, 1979); Regular columnist for *Anderson College News* ("The President's Corner"); Frequent contributor to *Vital Christianity, Youth, Christianity Today,* and other national periodicals.

Family Life: Married Geraldine Elizabeth Hurst on August 24, 1941; daughters: Rebecca, Constance, Kathleen; son, Eugene.

Contents

Part Three: Focus on Ministry

ESSAYS PRESENTED TO
Robert H. Reardon

Part I
Three Tributes

Robert H. Reardon:
A Personal Tribute
Gene W. Newberry

This tribute reflects forty-six years of friendship between Robert Reardon and me. Our careers have paralleled in ministry and education and, on reflection, I am surprised that we have agreed on so much and found common cause so often. All of it makes me feel good at this juncture in Bob's journey, and makes this writing easy. Thank God for this good friend and colleague.

Bob is a minister-educator with about equal weight on each of the two. If these two are at the bottom corners of the triangle, Christian (husband, parent, friend) is at the top, and integrity forms the gridwork across the center. No one places a finger on Bob as hard worker, creative, gutsy leader, ally in battle, responsible citizen, Christian brother and gentleman with class.

Forgive a personal word. I have been with Bob as fellow student, campus colleague, vacationer, traveler around the world, on boards and committees, and as a fellow church attender. It has been a joyous pilgrimage. Yet I would not psychoanalyze or pretend to plumb depths of character. He has sanctities and sanctuaries of thought and vocation, known to him and God, that I respect and admire. Bob flew away in personal retreat some days each year before college opened. What happened there in terms of devotion, meditation, reading, exercise, strategy, and hope is his own secret, but it seems to energize him for the year ahead.

I tell Bob that he operates by Christian instincts and that, fortunately, they are good ones. His vocation has peaks of insight that have taken Christian higher education in the Church of God to impressive heights. Part of that insight surely is picking colleagues (like Robert Nicholson). When Bob gets on a track he pushes and promotes tirelessly and carries his colleagues and institution with him. He is articulate and aggressive in pursuit of goals. He is relational, and even political, in the game. And he seems to enjoy every minute of it.

Looking for a secret to Reardon? Try roots. Through E. A. and Pearl Reardon, he is linked to pioneers and first-generation leaders of the Church of God. He is a preacher's kid, growing up in Chicago, Denver, and Anderson, listening to vigorous music and preaching, observing the excellencies and foibles of the parade of preachers, evangelists, and missionaries. He has memory and imagination that won't quit. The generations of Anderson College students will never forget his scintillating stories and, through him, will be linked to a rich heritage. Bob speaks with both tenderness and honesty about roots. He is proud of Eugene and Pearl Reardon and his brother, Willard.

When you ponder roots you think of Bob's immediate predecessor and mentor, John A. Morrison. Their story together is AC's story from 1917 to 1983. Morrison's practicality, sense of humor, and devotion to the church instructed Reardon. This was the foundation on which Bob built his educational basics. To these he added his own personal gifts of knowledge, preaching, and administration (following St. Paul's list). With these gifts he has done exactly the right

A Personal Tribute

thing—acknowledged, improved, dedicated, used them, and in so doing, has inspired and encouraged many youth.

Bob's least-known gift is music. He is an organist, and actually worked his way through Oberlin Graduate School of Theology as chapel organist. This must inspire him personally, and it surely has inspired students and others as he leads an impromptu singspiration in his home. He and Jerry share this gift together and make an impressive team.

You don't think of Bob without thinking of Jerry, his wife. Bob had the intelligence to pick the right girl. Or did she pick him? Her talents in teaching, preaching, and music are outstanding. The two made a great pastoral and educational couple. They raised a lovely family of four. And now there is a grandson who sends them looking for new sentiments and vocabulary. The Reardons knew how to make music together, travel together, and show us exemplary devotion.

Bob's roots have dictated his scholarship and writing. His master's thesis at Oberlin was titled "The Doctrine of the Church and the Christian Life in the Church of God Reformation Movement," an honest appraisal of history and doctrine. For the Church's centennial he wrote his reading of times and tides of the Church of God in *The Early Morning Light.* I hope he will be bringing out a book of his chapel sermons. At present he is writing a history of Anderson College and the saga of education. This will make interesting reading because, for thirty-six years, Bob has had a one-track mind: education—training the church's youth for various vocations. He was the campus's best critic; he was called to think institutionally and he did it. He was no-nonsense about Anderson College—about the budget, about required chapel, about excellence in teaching, about the physical plant, about accountability to the church, about sports, about Christian relationships. He was a money raiser, and could track a gift like a beagle tracks a rabbit. He could face tough, unpopular decisions. He had the vision of Anderson College being one of the top educational institutions in the Midwest. We think he has accomplished it.

The field in which Bob lived out his vocation was the church and his Christian faith. He is a popular preacher because he knows the Word and he knows life, and he can communicate both. He admits that he is hooked on preaching. Hear him and you know he loves it. He and Jerry pastored in Tipton and Loudonville, Ohio and Chester, Pennsylvania. For years he taught pastoral theology and homiletics at Anderson College and the School of Theology. He encouraged young preachers and inspired a love for church and ministry. I remember that project of fund raising for the new church in Chester. Bob and Jerry set the pattern for giving. They sold their Oldsmobile for one thousand dollars and led the way with their gift in that amount. I don't know, maybe it was a bicycle ministry after that. By the way, Bob has a great love for cars and wheels. Would he have been a car salesperson if he hadn't entered the ministry? Or would it have been politics?

Don't you like Bob's sense of humor? He can laugh at himself; he can laugh at life. All the fun he sees becomes grist for the homiletical mill. So most of his stories are not knee-slappers, but recognizable humor from the day's experience. One of the crazy ones he told me is about the young cowpoke riding out at sunrise. Soon he overtook an old prospector slogging along, leading his mule. The young guy reined up beside them and asked the old man if he knew how to dance. He said he didn't, and so the boy said he would teach him. Suddenly the young cowboy began to pepper the ground around him with his six-shooter. Of course, the old man did dance. The smart aleck had his fun, holstered his gun, and turned to ride off. The old prospector yelled, "Hey, bud," and the cowpoke turned and was looking down the barrel of a Winchester. He asked, "Did you ever kiss a mule?" "No," the boy said, "But I've always wanted to." Bob can make a point about manipulation and coercion out of a yarn like that.

8

A Personal Tribute

His best stories are about the daily rubbing and ribbing he encounters. Ask him about his mother riding the roller-coaster in Denver, or his looking up family ancestors in Ohio and Germany, or some political anecdote out of Washington. Ask him about losing his luggage in Calcutta or getting a stomach ache in Moscow. I hear Bob and I know that an interesting preacher must be a close observer of life and have a sense of humor. Link that with a love for the Word and the Church and the ability to communicate, and you have preaching at its best. Bob has become much more an expository preacher in his later years. That I commend because it shows him on the growing edge. He has the will and the drive to continue for many years.

Power to you, Robert.

Gene W. Newberry

The Three Rs . . .
Arlo F. Newell

Reading, writing, and arithmetic most often come to mind when we speak of the three Rs." The term is an attempt to focus attention on the basics in education: the ability to read with comprehension, write grammatically, and to understand mathematical computation.

However, the three Rs referred to in this editorial comment, while not unrelated to education, do not necessarily deal with these basics. *Remembering Robert Reardon* is what I want to write about.

My first introduction to Robert Reardon came in 1947, when he had been called from the pastorate in Chester, Pennsylvania, to serve as instructor at Anderson College. In Chester he preached to seventy-five people and at Anderson College he was my homiletics professor.

My recollection is not so much about the profound insights shared or the deep truths exegeted from Scripture, but about the inspiration of this young preacher-teacher. He was an *inspirer* of the highest order. His bearing as a man committed to Christ and the Church challenged me.

His keen intellect, refined through higher education at

Oberlin and continuing studies, made me desire to apply myself to the pursuit of education in preparation for the ministry. Even his style of dress and his personal carriage as a man touched the lives of the students in his classes. His influence has lived on through the years as this model for the ministry continues to teach through inspiration.

As an instructor, Robert Reardon became an *equipper* of ministers, preparing us to serve the Church. Not too far behind us at that time was the "anti-education" attitude in the ministry. Some believed that higher education was not really necessary for the ministry due to tendencies to depend upon human wisdom rather than divine revelation. Therefore, not every student was willing to be equipped educationally.

As a professor, Robert Reardon was demanding, expecting homiletics students to write out full sermon manuscripts. I still have one sermon written for his approval. It bears a personal handwritten note placed at the end of the introduction. It read, "Arlo, I would have been sound asleep by this time." Shocking? Not really. It helped me to see the tragedy of poor sermon preparation. While not guaranteeing that I would never repeat the unpardonable sin of dryness in my preaching, it did alert me to the need of diligent study in preparing to preach.

His purpose as an educator was not to make us feel good, but to equip us to serve God and the Church to the very best of our abilities. Preaching to him was not an ego trip, calling attention to the proclaimer, but an event pointing people to Christ, always giving hope that can be found nowhere else.

Reflections on the Reardon years cannot be isolated to the campus or the classroom. As a model for ministry, this professor became an *enabler* by sharing with the beginning pastor, that one just getting into the work of ministry. As associate minister in Akron, Indiana, with the late D. L. Slaybaugh, I recall having Robert Reardon for a series of meetings.

The Three Rs

One evening he was the dinner guest at the Newell home. With our first church, our first house, our first child, this was a real first; we were about overcome with fear and awe of this prestigious preacher.

To avoid unnecessary spills at the dinner table we served our firstborn cottage cheese, which she promptly rubbed in her hair. Embarrassed as we were, father Reardon put us at ease and enabled us to recognize that pastors and pastors's families are just about as normal as everyone else. His composure and understanding assured us that in the ministry we are still human and God expects no more.

Most significant in remembering is the fact that to the Church of God at large (as well as to me personally!) Robert Reardon has been a *stabilizer.* This does not mean that we have always agreed. I recall that on one occasion as a pastor I became greatly exercised in spirit over something that had happened on campus. So as not to forget, I immediately sat down and wrote a letter to the president. After addressing it and placing it in an envelope, I filed it in my desk drawer for two weeks. Taking it out, I read it again and then mailed it.

I waited impatiently for a response. Then came the letter with a rational, reasonable, intelligent answer to my inquiry. He did not sidestep the issue or attempt to convince me that my concern was unjustified. But as a Christian brother he shared with me insights about the problem that I did not fully understand and the reasoning that determined his action as president of the college.

Such has been true across the years as he has sought to stabilize both young and old in the life of this reformation movement. He has given young intellects who become impatient with the institutionalized life of the church a sense of balance, establishing them in the truths that do not change and that faith that will not fail. Older saints who have become critical, caustic, as well as genuinely concerned have regained a sense of trust and confidence when allowing this brother to share with them his love for Christ, the Word, and the Church.

13

I have watched him under fire in the General Assembly, criticized by the field, and misunderstood by the students; but in the midst of it all his attitude has stabilized my faith in God and has helped me work cooperatively in the Church to accomplish God's purpose in the world.

Remember Robert Reardon? How could anyone forget, when he has given so much to the church. While on the Executive Council as a pastor, I always enjoyed the annual reception held for guests from out of town at the Reardon residence.

After delicious refreshments, we would all gather in the living room to sing the songs of Zion. At the old pump organ was Dr. Reardon and playing the piano was his wife, Jerry. We sang songs such as "The Reformation Glory," "I Have a Home," "Beautiful," "On to the Goal," and "The Sunny Side of Life."

I remember not the harmony or the music, but the spirit as we shared together in fellowship and praise. Yes, we will always remember and continue to recognize our brother as a servant in Christ. We salute him for the past and pledge our prayers for the future.

A Tail and Its Kite

Val Clear

It was a pivotal event. Adam W. Miller was standing with a group of other young ministers. The year was 1915 and they were attending a missionary convention in the Bronx. J. T. Wilson, general manager of Gospel Trumpet Company, was the center of the circle and they pressed him with their question: "When is someone going to provide young ministers with training for gospel work?" He responded, "Gospel Trumpet Company is about to begin classes for workers and we would be glad to have you come to Anderson and join us."

This episode was not the first time in Church of God history that education was planned. The last issue of the *Gospel Trumpet* before D. S. Warner's death indicated that a committee would be meeting soon and that they would be discussing a school for training gospel workers. That was twenty years before Miller's question to Wilson. But significantly, in the issue after Warner's death, Enoch E. Byrum, the new editor, declared that there never would be such a school because education leads one to depend upon worldly wisdom rather than on God.

That discussion, that dichotomy, that choice never has been eliminated. It juxtaposes the movement between the false extremes of trusting God or trusting humankind, and much of our institutional history and sociology consist of the ways in which we have dealt with that pseudo-issue.

Can one serve God with maximum results on the foundation of God's guidance alone? Can one serve God with maximum results on the foundations of education alone? Put in those terms, the issue dissolves into amorphous confusion. Obviously, maximum results require both a full measure of God's leading *and* an adequate understanding of what for want of a better term we call secular culture.

But that has not been the posture of the Church of God reformation movement throughout most of its century of history. Rather, we have had a creative tension that has kept both extremes busy defending a position, and that tension has maximized results in both areas. Christian perceptions have sanctified human knowledge.

In such a setting of creative tension J. T. Wilson opened what later became Anderson College. It started on a simple enough level of part-time students and part-time faculty. It was a department (indeed, little more than a desk) of the Gospel Trumpet Company. A few students, mostly Gospel Trumpet workers, gathered in study groups with teachers—also workers—to search the Scriptures and a few related resources. In the beginning records were not kept because of the fear that if credit were given, seeds of pride would germinate into spiritual weeds. There was strong suspicion of Anderson Bible Training School. The General Ministerial Assembly set certain restrictions within which any school had to function, including a prohibition on giving course credit or conferring degrees.

This was relaxed in the mid-twenties, however. John A. Morrison had persuaded Russell Olt to move from his post as dean of Wilmington College, a Quaker school in Ohio, to ABTS. With Dean Olt came a dream of a well-rounded educational program, and one of the first things the two leaders did was to confer honorary doctor's degrees on key leaders of the movement, with particular attention to leaders of the opposition to formal education.

The strategy worked. Only a few years later Anderson Bible Training School had become Anderson College and Theological Seminary and it was giving four-year liberal-arts degrees. A few years later the liberal-arts degree was the only one offered, even for ministerial students. Thus was created the institution that we know today as Anderson College, to which was added the Graduate School of Theology in 1950. Now let us turn our attention from history to sociology.

That casual conversation on the steps in the Bronx in 1915 is certainly one of the most crucial in Church of God sociology. In retrospect we can see that it led to the implementation of a strong desire for preparation for the ministry, and it brought into the lifeblood of the movement persons of the caliber of Adam W. Miller, a highly respected scholar. The creation of the educational thrust set the direction of social change throughout these sixty-eight years and without a doubt the die is firmly cast for future developments.

Recall the setting. The evangelical world was about to be torn apart in bitter conflict between science and religion. Evolutionists were seen as educated bad guys and their badness was the result of their education. Seminaries were seen as hotbeds of rational thought and higher criticism, which were regarded as synonymous with agnosticism. Most churches spent more time fighting Christian educators than they did fighting with unbelievers. Fundamentalism as a movement was born about 1910 and all who accepted the fundamentals believed that education was a threat to the truth. That the positions they fought (such as higher criticism) are now embraced unquestioningly by the New Right does not alter the historical fact that a bitter struggle took place within the Church between those who accepted rationality and learning and those who rejected such views.

So ABTS was born in controversy. Two persons in particular were centers of the struggle because they tended to function on the basis of reason more than on mystical guidance, although as seasoned members of the movement they made verbal genuflections to Spirit guidance on cue. These two leaders were Russell R. Byrum and Walter S. Haldeman.

These two extremely important people have been chronicled elsewhere by John W. V. Smith and Robert H. Reardon, who knew them well; so let me merely assert here that Byrum and Haldeman came into academe as men committed to truth wherever it was encountered, and they called attention to the fact that truth is sometimes found in strange places, such as in the teachings of philsophers and theologians who never did subscribe to the *Gospel Trumpet*. This was regarded as heretical by some and it led to the ouster of Byrum from the faculty of Anderson College. It is to be noted that he said that they could put him out of Anderson College and Theological Seminary and out of the General Ministerial Assembly, but they could not put him out of the Church of God. He continued to worship and teach a vigorous Sunday school class in Park Place Church of God until shortly before his death.

One of the most moving moments in General Assembly history came a few years ago when he was brought in for an award and the ministers and lay members stood in respect a thousand strong and gave a thundering apology to one of the great figures in Church of God heritage. The battles of secular versus spiritual were forgotten. But after a lifetime of torture, scars are deep and Russell Byrum, though reconciled, was never fully restored.

Haldeman was crucified on the "Nature or Nurture" cross. In the early 1930s a group of Ohio ministers became perturbed because of his teaching, which implied that Christian education in the church is important because we can teach our children to accept Christ by proper instruction. Those Ohio ministers denied that that kind of conditioning could lead a person to Christ. Does that sound a little silly? Well, the reason it sounds silly in 1983 is that Walter S. Haldeman won the battle fifty years ago. He never knew, even when he died, that he had won. It was a subtle victory and few of his contemporaries were ever aware of how his position would eventually permeate the movement.

Both Byrum and Haldeman were possible only because Anderson College provided a cocoon in which they could metamorphose. They had risen from the same subculture as other Church of God leaders (their families had followed Warner before the men were born) but somewhere along the line each had acquired a taste for knowledge and both adapted and recycled the greater culture for Church of God palates. Through this cross-fertilization they innoculated students with ideas that later would emerge in pulpits and camp meetings throughout the Church of God reformation movement. What Byrum and Haldeman placed in their course outlines multiplied geometrically as students became pastors and lay leaders in churches and assemblies. To use a familiar biblical figure of speech, they leavened the whole lump.

No review of social change in the Church of God would be adequate without attention to John A. Morrison and Russell Olt. They were an unusually matched pair. Their traits and skills dovetailed. Without the other, either would have been a rather ordinary person. Together, they were phenomenal.

J. A. Morrison was at heart the perfect pragmatist. I once asked him if he would accept a hundred dollars from a bar owner on Main Street. "Of course," he said. "Money in itself has no moral value." Dean Olt, on the other hand, was a person of delicate and profound principles. He almost lost his Anderson College job in the early 1930s when he walked at the head of the procession down Meridian Street in which the union was opposing General Motors and trying to organize the plants. Olt was progressive on every social issue, while Morrison was usually conservative.

But on educational issues they stood firm. I came to Anderson College to teach in 1947, right after the war. I had been openly a Christian pacifist throughout the war but I am sure that if someone had protested my appointment, they would have listened, then gone ahead as planned. Academic freedom was crucial. I recall one sensitive incident in which this happened.

One of my colleagues, Dr. John O. Carrington, had extravagant appreciation for Franklin Delano Roosevelt and any other Democrat you might happen to mention, but little good to say about Dwight Eisenhower or any Republican. Since he taught American history, this was a noticeable bias. An influential member of the Board of Trustees went to Morrison and demanded that Carrington be fired. When Carrington heard of this he stormed in to Morrison's office and threw a sheet of paper on the desk. "There," he fumed. "I refuse to stay another day under pressure from the administration of this college! "

"When did you hear about this, John?" the president asked. Carrington hedged but stood his ground. "John," Morrison continued, "that trustee came to me three months ago. What I told him was that he had absolutely nothing to do with who is hired and who is fired around here except for the president. If he doesn't like the way I am running the place he can fire me, but no one else. Now, go back to your classes and teach. That's why I am here, to keep you teaching." That same attitude was expressed in my own case when the American Guard, a predecessor of the John Birch Society, launched a witch-hunt against me in the 1950s. From the very beginning Anderson College built an excellent record of academic freedom and it is only because of that traditional posture that its influence has been so pervasive throughout the entire Church of God reformation movement.

A Tail and Its Kite

During the Watchman on the Wall agitation in the mid-1940s the college came under attack but it had the rare luxury of company; virtually every general agency and executive was the target of the L. Earl Slacum pen. Brother Slacum has since told me that he regrets the way in which he handled his protest but he feels that his points were well taken. The charge was worldliness and part of the objection involved the Anderson College curriculum. There was too much of the world and too little of Christ. For the most part, Anderson College stood its ground, as if to change would be to self-incriminate. The college joined the other agencies in holding the line, even to the point of persuading loyal alumni to attend when the crucial vote was to be taken, both in the Indiana Assembly and in the General Ministerial assembly.

Earlier I implied that the appearance of Anderson College has been the most important development in the Church of God reformation movement, at least since Warner's death in 1895. Let me be explicit.

In 1951 I did a study in which I compared the list of pastors with the list of alumni of Anderson College. At that time more than half of the pastors had been students at Anderson College, and they tended to hold the largest congregations. Even today, Anderson College graduates pastor a significant number of churches in the movement.

The impact of the college on the subculture of the Church of God is tremendous and, I would guess, not readily noticed. At several points in our history we have had to choose between a radically conservative position (read fundamentalism if you wish) and a more temperate position. We have always come out in the middle of the road, orthodox and practical. We have rejected extremism in every crisis in which we have had to make a choice. Our colleges are to be credited for this, especially Anderson College.

The curriculum at Anderson College is called liberal arts because when it is functioning at its best, it liberates. That is why Anderson College has had so major an impact upon the Church of God. The traditional Bible school approach, it seems to me, is of only limited usefulness. The minister who knows only the Bible is woefully incompetent. The gospel requires an earthly relevance in order for it to be fully expressed, and a liberal arts context does this with the most efficiency. Anderson College has set the pattern by which all Church of God institutions of higher education enhance our biblical heritage with secular perceptions relevant to the world of 1983.

I see clearly that the Church of God reformation movement has its uniqueness, its personality, its way of life, primarily because of the filter-effect that Anderson College has performed on the lifeblood that has flowed into the Church through the young people who have had direct or indirect impact from the college.

This thought brings us to another pivotal day in the history of the Church of God: September 1, 1947. On that date Robert H. Reardon first appeared on the payroll. Not that it was much of a payroll—he got about twenty-one hundred dollars for the year. J. A. Morrison had felt that he needed to pick a successor, train him, test him, and see if he could fly. It was a successful experiment. The Board nominated Reardon as president and the General Ministerial Assembly ratified the choice. He followed a predecessor who, at the time of his retirement, had been one of the country's longest-serving college presidents.

When Reardon took over, the ship had come through several stormy seas but waters were calm (except for chronic financial problems) and ready for a vigorous run into the future.

I cannot write of those years with objectivity. They are also my own story and Robert Reardon has always been a part of it. We have shared the most intimate of hopes and heartbreaks, both victories and defeats, families and friends for almost fifty years. We knelt together at the altar for

A Tail and Its Kite

ordination and years later at my wife's funeral I asked him to express the love of her circle of friends. He is in a very real sense a part of me.

At his retirement ceremony a panoply of achievements was recited including the indisputable fact that every building now on the campus was dedicated after he joined the staff.

What needs to be said more loudly than that, though, is that the intangible part of his legacy is much more important than the physical plant, impressive as it is. He was not just a money-raiser, as many presidents are, but he gave key personal leadership in curriculum and in the formation of the ambience on campus. Without the latter, Anderson College would be just another school.

The college community is as varied as two thousand different individuals can make it, and no individual can be fully representative. But the model toward which the institution inclines is a Christian young person who sincerely seeks to live a life committed to actualizing the gospel through the life of a responsible citizen. This includes a fulfilling family relationship, active community involvement, and professional competence as minimum Christian obligations.

During the 1960s and 1970s church colleges around the country discontinued compulsory chapel. Robert Reardon was pressured by students and faculty to do so but he refused. Despite demonstrations and disruptions in chapel services, he retained on Anderson College campus a tradition of religion as a regular part of the life of the individual and of the scholarly community. Had he given in to that pressure, the contemporary climate on campus of responsible Christian involvement might not have been.

I came to Anderson College in August 1936. One of the first persons I met was Robert Reardon's father, E. A. Reardon, pastor of Park Place Church of God. He was a remarkable person: straight as a pole physically and morally, Irish to the core, progressive in most regards, and an unusually warm shepherd. I was struggling with a career choice. He gave me the best advice I have ever had. "Val, the only way to full and lasting satisfaction is to pick an institution and tie yourself to it as a tail to a kite."

When I answered God's call and committed myself to full-time service, it was to preach. I thought that was the only way open. But I soon realized that God did not want me preaching. That is when I met Carl Kardatzke. His impact upon the direction of change in the Church of God has not yet been duly appreciated. He changed the course of many lives and laid the foundation for strong vocational tracks in our colleges. The concept of servanthood in such fields as public-school education, nursing, social work, criminal justice, business, medicine, and law is accepted now but only because of Carl Kardatzke's pioneering ministry.

Carl was chair of the Department of Education at Anderson College and he sold a startling viewpoint. Preaching is not the only way to serve God. Missionaries do, too. And public school teachers, he said. The latter was said with emphasis and conviction and he repeated it until he got through to me that teaching is for some a calling as authentic and as valid as pastoring or serving as a missionary.

What a liberation that was! Not only teaching, but farming and truck driving and just about any vocation could become a ministry, a committed service to God. Just let God plan it, he said, and for you it is a ministry. That opened the way to the broad vocational spectrum in our colleges today.

Back to Bob Reardon. He left a pastorate in Chester, Pennsylvania, in 1947 to join the college staff. Someone said to him. "But how can you leave the ministry to go to the college?" The preceding paragraphs answer that question. His effective ministry at the college, the leadership he has provided, the sensitive relationships with generations of students—these are rich endorsements of his decision to invest his ministry among the youth of the Church of God. Nowhere else could he, given the gifts that are his, have had

A Tail and Its Kite

so fruitful a ministry.

And his father's kite tail? Bob exemplifies it nicely. He picked the institution, tied himself to it inextricably, and they both have flown well together.

Valorous B. Clear

Part II

Heritage
and
Theological Studies

What the Church
Does with Its Eyes
Gilbert W. Stafford

Some places of worship make it easy for us to know what to do with our eyes. Perhaps it is the cross that draws our attention, or a stained-glass window, or an architectural feature that inevitably directs our eyes in a certain direction. But other places of worship make it difficult for us to know what to do with them. Shall we gaze at the worship leader? Shall we look at the choir members? If there is a transparent window, we might turn our eyes in that direction. Sometimes, we close them, simply because we can find no suitable visual focus as we worship.[1] The reason so many worshipers stare at the printed words of a hymn even though they know them by heart may be due to their frustration as to what they should do with their eyes.

Just as we do various things with our eyes during worship, even so the historical church as a whole handles its eyes of faith in a variety of ways. What the Church does with its eyes greatly influences the way it functions. Sometimes the Church turns its eyes backward to former glory; sometimes forward to a joyous goal; sometimes upward to that which is awesomely real; sometimes downward to that which is shockingly tangible; sometimes inward to a personal awareness; and sometimes outward to a challenging mission. Indeed, one of the ways that the history of the Church could be written is by identifying what it has done with its eyes throughout the centuries of its existence.

THE BACKWARD LOOK

No small part of the Church has from time to time turned its eyes primarily backward to gaze at some former glory, whether it be the glory of the old-time religion, or the glory of some sort of primitive purity, or the glory of some kind of former power, perhaps either spiritual, political, or intellectual. The past is so easily idealized and romanticized that it serves as a convenient way of escape from the hard realities of the present.

In central Indiana there is a delightful 1836 Hoosier community known as Conner Prairie Pioneer Settlement. Conner Prairie is a museum program of Earlham College, the aim of which is to present to the public a replica of 1836 Hoosier life as close to the actual life-style, language, and customs of that year as possible. When the museum was started, the men who worked as the 1836 citizens of Conner Prairie wore beards. But after a while historical researchers discovered that 1836 Hoosier men were for the most part clean shaven; consequently, all the men had to shave off their beards—a decision that caused no small displeasure among those who found their Conner Prairie employment an excellent excuse for letting their whiskers grow. Devotion to the past had dictated the painful decision of the present. That kind of earnest commitment to the past makes it easy for one who spends a day in the settlement to begin to feel as though the calendar really has been turned backward.

This is also the way the church from time to time and from place to place functions. Its eyes are turned to former glories, and whenever one spends much time in that type of church, the experience is primarily one of reveling in the past. In fact, one is jolted by the discontinuity of time that exists between this kind of church and the everyday world. Upon entering or leaving such a Christian community, it is as though one enters or leaves a religious museum of a past age. The religious life of some Christian people is chiefly an ongoing routine of existing in two calendar worlds, one having to do with their particular religious museum and the other with the here and now.

To be sure, there is an important difference between making a fetish of the past, on the one hand, and bringing that which is of lasting value from the past into the present, on the other. Anything in the past that is of value is valuable not because of its pastness but because of its relevance in the present. It is not its age that makes it valuable but its truthfulness.[2]

THE FORWARD LOOK

While some sections of the Church turn their eyes upon past glories, other sections turn them primarily forward to a future happening or development, the possibilities of which are as diverse as (1) the anticipated establishment of the historical Church in some sort of structural unity, (2) the unfolding of prophetic events on the divine calendar, and (3) the eventual realization of some social goal such as the abolition of war as a means of dealing with international conflict. Ecumenical Christianity,[3] Prophetic Christianity,[4] and Pacifist Christianity,[5] though very different in their respective concerns and approaches, are alike in their common devotion to a futuristic goal.[6] These three forms of Christianity are certainly not the only examples of the Church turning its eyes forward. One is reminded of Liberationist Christianity, which seeks to bring in a completely new social order to replace the traditional Western system, especially Western capitalism and democracy;[7] and Utopian Christianity, which commits itself to the establishment of communities of perfect love and peace.[8] The history of the Church records an abundance of prophetic miscalculations, disappointed idealists, disillusioned goal seekers and broken dreams—all the product of turning the eyes altogether toward a future goal that is distorted by the absence of other equally important considerations. It is not the concerns themselves that are being called into question here but the lack of balance that *sometimes* prevails.

THE UPWARD LOOK

Another option that the Church sometimes chooses as it decides what to do with its eyes is that of turning them primarily upward to a transcendent reality. Those who take this option are in some sense overwhelmed by the presence of the Divine, who is experienced either as an awesome reality into which one is mystically united, or as a joyous presence that envelopes one, or finally as an objective transcendence that causes one to stand in humble respect. Whereas mystical union with the awesome God is necessarily an individualized occurrence, the experience of being enveloped by the gladdening presence of the transcendent can be either an individual or a communal one. In fact, the community of believers claiming to be enveloped by the Spirit often finds itself testifying among themselves about the blessedness of the divine presence communally experienced. However, this kind of group phenomenon also encourages the possibility of individualized, private experiences of the transcendent, the authentication of which is fully dependent on the testimony of the possessor of the experience. Persons whose eyes are turned primarily toward the transcendent are prone to develop a God-and-me attitude, devoid of checks, whether those of Scripture, the Church, or of reason. This danger is characteristic not only of individuals, but also of "ecclesial communities"[9] that make special claims about being enveloped by the divine presence. The confidence of authenticity arising out of the

What the Church Does with Its Eyes

experience itself makes it very difficult for those who are outsiders to be heard as they apply the check of Scripture, or the check of the combined understanding of the universal Church, or the check of reason guided by faith. As we can see, the responses made to the transcendent reality vary all the way from the mystic's absolute silence to the modern charismatic's exuberant tongues of praise; all the way from the Calvinist's logical explication of the absolute sovereignty of God to the Pentecostalist's emphasis on being "slain in the Spirit";[10] all the way from the more exclusivistic attitude of, We really know God whereas you only think you do, to the more inclusivistic attitude of, We really know God and hope to lead you to him also.

THE DOWNWARD LOOK

The fourth possibility that some sections of the Church choose is that of turning their eyes primarily downward to the hard realities of human life. Often the turning of the eyes in this direction is an overt reaction to those who have too strongly emphasized the upward gaze at the expense of social responsibility. Whereas the former are moved by their own personal awareness of God, the latter are moved by their awareness of humankind's need for redemptive help. They give this help through such modes as social activism, medical missionary work, compassionate deeds of kindness, and the ministry of advocacy on behalf of those who are powerless to gain whatever it is they need. Since there is no end to human need in the world as we know it, for the Church to fix its eyes solely on the plight of the human order is a guarantee for either emotional breakdown or spiritual abandonment of the cause altogether.

A research hospital in Boston admits only terminally ill patients. An acquaintance of mine who visited that hospital with some regularity, claimed that he could immediately distinguish the newer doctors and nurses from longer-term ones: the newcomers were cheerful, positive, and full of energy; the longer-term personnel were downhearted, sluggish, and haggard. The percentage of successful operations and treatments was so low that it was extremely difficult for doctors and nurses to maintain a healthy attitude toward their work. Likewise, the gaze of faith that is solely downward makes for haggard churches and haggard Christians. They are somewhat like the overly devoted parent who lovingly cares for children twenty-four hours a day without any respite. The usual result is oppressive tension that negates the anticipated exuberance of fulfilling home life.

THE INWARD LOOK

Another possible focus for the eyes of the Church is the inward look. The Wesleyan/Holiness tradition is particularly prone to turn in upon the self and to concentrate on matters of internal assurance as to whether one is completely right with God. Preachers who have replaced the gospel of Christ with the gospel of internal assurance often question their congregations about their status before God, making inquiries like the following: Is there a *secret* sin that is lurking in the deeper recesses of the heart? Is there *complete* dedication to the cause of Christ? Is there *any* word, thought, or deed that is not controlled by the Holy Spirit?[11] Those individuals and churches that concentrate fanatically on the look inward are sure to develop a neurotic preoccupation about minor issues—the individuals being overly concerned about such matters as fleeting thoughts, and congregations being unduly captivated by such issues as the enforcement of detailed dress codes. These kinds of holy minutiae sap the spiritual and emotional strength of the Church, producing legalistic fellowships and rigid individuals whose major worry is the status of their own salvation.

Another way the Church has of looking inward is at its institutional life. Continuous attention to the inner workings of the organizational dimension of the Church's life (e.g., endless bylaws revisions, continuous self-studies, constant

What the Church Does with Its Eyes

rearrangement of institutional patterns of operation) can atrophy the effectiveness of the Church in much the same way that legalism and rigidity about spiritual life do. Both, though in different ways, are forms of religious navel worship. This turning in upon the self causes the Church to return to a fetal position of total dependency rather than develop into an upright positon of mature responsibility for the spread of the gospel. While it is true that poorly structured institutions certainly do hinder the spread of the Good News, it is equally true that carefully crafted institutions do not in and of themselves guarantee effectiveness in its spread.

THE OUTWARD LOOK

The final possibility for the Church's use of its eyes is to turn them primarily outward to the mission of the Church, thereby concentrating all of its energies on the accomplishment of that task. Passionate distortions of the Church's missionary agenda are illustrated by such phenomena as the cultishness of some Christian television programming, the practice of a truncated evangelism that has no adequate education for discipleship, and the promulgation of a missionary triumphalism that seeks to conquer the world or save a nation through conversion to Christianity, so that in actuality the preaching of the gospel comes mainly to have a utilitarian and nationalistic character to it. Getting on with the task, reaching the goal, doing the job, winning the day, being the best and the biggest—these are the rallying points for those ecclesial communities that have almost exclusively turned their eyes outward. A distorted emphasis on the outward gaze makes for competitiveness, boastfulness, and humiliation. In our town a certain church has what it calls the Goat Bus, which is driven by the bus captain who brought in the fewest Sunday school passengers the previous week.

A few years ago, the pastor of a nationally known super church is reported to have told some bankers, who at first had refused his church a loan, that if they did not come through with the loan, he would see to it that they would suffer in the millennium. He reported to them that the Lord had already promised that he (the pastor) was to rule over that particular geographical area in the coming dispensation. Since he would be in power, and they out of power, he was going to make it hard on them unless the loan was granted. The clincher of the story is that the bankers changed their minds and loaned the money!

ILLUSTRATIVE SONGS

If a theme song for each of these types of Christian churches were chosen, the following might be appropriate: Those whose eyes are primarily turned backward might longingly sing the happy chorus " 'Tis the old-time religion, and it's good enough for me! " Those with eyes primarily turned forward might choose Isaac Watts's hopeful hymn "Jesus shall reign wher-e'r the sun/Does his successive journeys run;/His kingdom spread from shore to shore,/Till moon shall wax and wane no more." Those with eyes turned upward might select the awesome words by Walter C. Smith, "Immortal, invisible, God only wise,/In light inaccessible hid from our eyes,/Most blessed, most glorious, the Ancient of Days,/Almighty, victorious, thy great name we praise." Christian people with eyes turned downward might sing Washington Gladden's compassionate "O Master, let me walk with thee,/In lowly paths of service free;/Tell me thy secret, help me bear/The strain of toil, the fret of care." The song that those with eyes turned primarily inward might choose is Elisha A. Hoffman's introspective "Is Your All on the Altar?" the first stanza of which warns "You have longed for sweet peace, and for faith to increase,/And have earnestly, fervently pray'd;/But you cannot have rest, or be perfectly blest/Until all on the altar is laid." Finally, those whose eyes are primarily turned outward in missionary earnestness might select "I Cannot Be Idle" by William J. Henry, the fourth stanza of which declares "I cannot be idle, no time for repose, /My resting shall be over there,/Where all of the faithful in heaven above,/A crown of bright glory shall wear."

Of course, no ecclesial community belongs strictly within any one of these types, but the *obvious* differences between the many sections of the church, both past and present, do suggest that there are fundamentally different directions in which the eyes of faith are looking. My students in Christian worship class at Anderson School of Theology become keenly aware of this when on our annual field trip we visit five or six churches at worship, all in one day. Often the schedule includes services at Episcopalian, Presbyterian, Pentecostal, Roman Catholic, Black Disciples of Christ, and Greek Orthodox churches. Almost without exception, students begin the day with great anticipation but by mid-afternoon they have headaches, are nauseated, and are commenting about the emotional difficulty involved in making the transitions from one kind of worship to others vastly different. The reality of the varied directions in which the eyes of Christian faith are focused is vividly illustrated to them in one day's time.

THE NEW TESTAMENT FOCUS

What, then, shall we do with our eyes of faith? Shall we choose one of the six options previously set forth? The tenor of this essay up to this point certainly suggests that none of these is adequate either in and of itself or in combination with any or all of the others. The fact of the matter is that one can find in the New Testament sufficient evidence for building a biblical rationale for all of these directions but not for any one of them alone. The simple yet profound truth is that the eyes of the church in the New Testament were focused on the person and work of Jesus Christ, whose life was the epitome of all the truthfulness of the past, the revelation of the future consummation of all history, the incarnation of the transcendent God himself among us

37

(Emmanuel),[12] the ministry of compassionate love for the whole world plagued by sin, the reality of unbroken communion with eternal Godhead, and the announcement of Good News to all peoples. The eyes of Christ were turned backward, forward, upward, downward, inward, and outward, not in succession but simultaneously. The backward gaze was oriented to the future[13] and the future gaze was focused by the past. The upward look penetrated the needs of the world and the downward look was through the eyes of the transcendent God in all of his immanent love. His inward sensitivity was oriented to the ends of the world and his outward mission was the continuation of his inward life.

What happened at Pentecost is that the church whose eyes of faith were focused *on* Christ became the church whose eyes of faith were focused *by* Christ. The church of Pentecost was given Christly eyes. They were simultaneously turned backward to the biblical history of redemption, forward in joyous anticipation of God's eternal newness, upward in worship of the God who was pouring out his Spirit abundantly, downward to the realities of human life, inward to the personal confirmation of the divine work of grace, and outward to the fields white unto harvest.

THE ONGOING CHALLENGE OF BEING THE CHURCH[14]

As one reads the history of the Church since the Day of Pentecost, one finds that divisions, antagonisms and acts of mutual ostracism are a disturbing part of the story. Is this the continuation of the church of Pentecost? Even though I am among those theological analysts who attribute in part these facts of the Church's history to sin, I think that they are also partly attributable to the desire to please God. One predominant issue leading to division in the course of church history is this: How ought God's Church to function? Every new ecclesial community has come into existence with the conviction that its own particular *modus operandi* was significantly more harmonious with God's expectation for the Church than that of other communities of Christian faith. The nineteenth- and twentieth-century unity movements are likewise characterized by the same predominant concern: How ought God's Church to function?[15] That continues being the challenge for the contemporary church as it deals with both new divisions as well as new attempts at unity. This challenge is being met in a variety of ways with some contemporaries saying that what the Church needs is a return to the tried and tested ways of the past, while others say that the only salvation for the Church is for it to venture daringly into the new and unknown. Still others claim that the greatest need for the Church is to be overwhelmed by the presence of God, while others urge it to identify more closely with the suffering of humanity. Some proclaim that the answer to any floundering in the Church is to be found in the spread of "heartfelt, know-so" Christianity, while others say that the answer is to be found in a more intensive missionary thrust.[16]

The challenge that faces the Church today, however, will never be met with adequacy as long as we conceive of ourselves as a collection of churches with competing emphases rather than as the one universal community of Christ, in need of the decisive work of God manifested at Pentecost. The one Christ has but one Church vivified by only one Spirit. The critical issue, then, is whether the contemporary church is willing to throw open its life to the same Pentecostal outpouring of the Holy Spirit that is reported in Acts 2. The Acts 2 outpouring is as available to the church of the present century as it was to the first-century church. Just as there is no living Lord of the Church other than the Christ of the New Testament, even so there is no Holy Spirit other than the one manifested on the Day of Pentecost. The divine question posed to the Church in every age and place is this: Have you opened yourselves as the community of faith to the vivification of the Holy Spirit poured out at Pentecost? When the Church desires the vivification of the Holy Spirit as earnestly as the original church of 120 did, it will be given the Christly focus on its being, relationships, and mission. The backward, forward, upward, downward, inward, outward foci will then no longer be options about which the churches compete, but rather the full complement of marks by which the ongoing church of Pentecost is identifiable.

DISTINGUISHING MARKS OF THE CHURCH

The question as to how one can distinguish the true church from its counterfeits has been widely discussed throughout the history of Christianity. Traditionally, Eastern Orthodoxy has held that the chief mark of the Church is its unbroken tradition of the gospel;[17] Roman Catholicism has stressed that the chief mark is its apostolic continuity through an unbroken chain of ordination from the first century to the present; classical Protestantism (Lutheranism and Calvinism) has taught that the marks of the Church are the Word being truly preached and the Sacraments being rightly administered;[18] and spiritualistic Protestantism (such as Quakers and Pentecostalists) has maintained that the mark of the Church is what one Methodist scholar has called "Spirit-centered freedom."[19]

Ecclesiologist J. Robert Nelson tells in his book *Criterion for the Church* about a meeting of a theological commission on Faith and Order in which one participant had stressed the point that a true church must possess the classically defined elements of the Word, the Sacraments, order, and discipline. "Whereupon," he writes, another participant "responded wryly that the church across the street from him had possessed all these—and still it died!" Nelson goes on to comment that "the fault lay not in having these ecclesiastical marks, of course, but in having them in form rather than in force."[20]

William Barclay has observed that "as Acts sees it, the mark of a Church is the presence of the Spirit."[21] To be sure there are traditional, institutional, and confessional implications of the presence of the Spirit, but the point is that neither the tradition, the institution, nor the confession, be it ever so right, is in and of itself the mark of the Church; rather, the once-and-for-all Pentecostal effusion is the mark without which all traditions, institutions, and confessions are but empty husks of that which is not there.

All of the traditional marks as expounded by their respective exponents remind us of critically important matters for serious consideration, but all of them together are insufficient apart from Pentecostal empowerment, for identifying the Church. Pentecostal empowerment brings about several results in the life of the Church: it contemporizes the biblical gospel and continually transforms all who believingly and trustingly hear it; it purifies not only the ordained ministry but the whole people of God for their daily service; it vivifies the preaching of the biblical Word of God and makes it "sharper than any two-edged sword" (Heb. 4:12);[22] it liberates the people of God from sinful bondage, focusing their freedom not on their own individual rights and joys, but on the worldwide missionary endeavor of the Church, and in so doing transforms them into sacramental communicators of the grace of God.

The critical questions, then, for identifying the Church are these:

1. Is the gospel of the biblical tradition being faithfully preached, taught, and lived in the power of the Holy Spirit?
2. Are the lives of those listening to the biblical gospel being transformed by it?
3. Are their lives being purified in word, thought, and deed?
4. Is the worshiping church a sacrament of grace in the world? Are individual believers sacraments of grace? That is, do they communicate God's redeeming, sanctifying, and keeping power to others?
5. Is the Church earnestly pursuing its divine mission to the uttermost parts of the world?

As we study the Book of Acts, we see that the answers to all of these questions are in the affirmative. The marks of the Church as traditionally set forth are insufficient for demarcating the Church. The *sine qua non* for identifying the Church is the mark of Pentecost as it is set forth in the Book of Acts. Clark Pinnock, professor of systematic theology at McMaster Divinity School, and noted evangelical scholar, writes about "opening the church to the Charismatic dimension." As a Baptist, he laments,

> My own denomination suffers as much from dead orthodoxy as it does from lifeless liberalism, yet it is deathly afraid of what might happen if the Spirit came sweeping over us. In our pews sit hundreds of discouraged saints. They are not lusting for existential benefits beyond those in Christ. They are simply thirsting for more of his fullness and for greater warmth from the spiritual fire within.[23]

He then goes on to say that "it is not a *doctrine* of the Spirit that we need, but a *movement* of the Spirit, pervading and filling us, setting our convictions on fire."[24] While I think that Pinnock is overstating the case when he says that it is not a doctrine that we need (as a systematic theologian he, of course, sees the need for good doctrinal understandings of the person and work of the Holy Spirit), I think that he is not overstating the case at all when he speaks of the great need for the Church to be open to the Spirit's movement. From time to time we hear calls for a new Pentecost, but God has promised no new Pentecost any more than he has promised a new Messiah. Just as the one Messiah has come and will return, even so the one outpouring of the Holy Spirit has been given, and God has never withdrawn it. The wind-and-fire of Pentecost was as available in the spiritually dark fifteenth century as it was in the first; it is as available now as it was when the original 120 were gathered in Jerusalem. W. T. Conner, an evangelical theologian, has set forth in no uncertain terms the cruciality of Pentecost.

What the Church Does with Its Eyes

He writes,

> Pentecost was just as essential for the realization in the lives of men of the values of the gospel as was Calvary and the resurrection. Without the death and resurrection of Jesus there would be no gospel. Without Pentecost there would be no gospel as far as our apprehension and experience are concerned.[25]

Whereas Calvary and the Resurrection established the reality of our salvation, Pentecost established the community of our salvation. The reality of salvation is at the center of the community of salvation, and the community of salvation is the agency for extending the reality of salvation. In conversion our eyes are turned in faith on Christ; because of Pentecost they are focused through Christ on the world.

EFFECTS OF THE PENTECOSTAL EFFUSION[26]

We have already said that the Pentecostal experience of the Holy Spirit turns the Church's eyes of faith backward, forward, upward, downward, inward, and outward all at the same time, and that this is the *sine qua non* of the ongoing church of Pentecost. But what are some of the concrete evidences of such a multidirectional view? On the basis of the Book of Acts, we can say that the ongoing church of Pentecost has the following characteristics:

1. A truly ecumenical community of believers is established which is devoted (a) to the study of the apostles' teaching; (b) to the interpersonal experience of being common participants in a new divine reality; (c) to the breaking of bread for both physical as well as spiritual nourishment;[27] and (d) to earnest prayer. (See Acts 4:31.) Furthermore, in the church of Pentecost, miraculous occurrences announce the inbreaking of the new era of God's reign. Mutual help, support, and sharing within the community are the order of the day. Gladness, praise, and joy are predominant traits of the community, even in times of extreme trial. (See especially the account of Paul and Silas in Acts 16:22-25.) In fact, the

43

quality of the community's life is so divinely beautiful that it wins the favor of the outside world.[28] To be sure, there are instances of persecution, but the persecution takes place because the public is angry at the claims of the Gospel and not because of the Church's quality of life.

2. Ecclesiastical conversion to Christ is normative, as is seen in Acts 2:41, "And there were added that day about three thousand souls"; "And the Lord added to their number day by day those who were being saved"(2:47); and "The number of the disciples multiplied greatly in Jerusalem" (6:7). We find in Acts that people are converted to Christ and to his Church simultaneously. Conversion to Christ in isolation from his ecumenical community is not in the spirit of Pentecost.

3. Worship leads to evangelism and evangelism leads to worship. Throughout the Book of Acts one sees this mutual relationship between the two. The upward and inward experience in worship is based on the backward and forward relatedness to God's action in history and leads to the downward and outward movement of service to human need and evangelism to the ends of the earth. But the process does not stop when persons have been converted. The goal of evangelism is that the converted might be brought into the fellowship of divine worship, beginning here and now to participate with the universal congregation of believers both on earth and in heaven as they praise and adore the triune God. Robert Coleman, in his exposition of the Book of Revelation lifts up this close connection between evangelism and worship. He writes,

> One wants only to bow before Him and, with all the universe, join in the praise of the Lamb. In this holy communion, our love unites with His, quickening a desire to mount the housetops and herald His name to the ends of the earth and to the farthest star.[29]

44

What the Church Does with Its Eyes

The God of creation and redemption who is worshiped in heaven is the God whom those who are evangelized come to worship even now, and on the basis of their worship they in turn become evangelists of the Good News.

4. Holy Spirit baptism is the power for the entire sanctification of the believer's life so that nothing whatsoever is able to turn him or her away from devotion to the Lord. It is significant that Acts records the martyrdom of Stephen, who being full of the Holy Spirit (Acts 7:55) was so completely given over to the service of the Lord that all the mad fury of his antagonists, and finally their public stoning of him could not distract him from faith in Christ. In the midst of their madness he saw the glory of God (7:55). As the stones came at him, he prayed, "Lord, do not hold this sin against them" (7:60). Stephen is an example of the entire sanctification made possible by the Pentecostal work of the Holy Spirit. When the Spirit is allowed to do his sufficient work in believers, they pass the point of no return when nothing whatsoever will cause them to shun Christ, and they are able to say *Maranatha* ("Our Lord, Come!")[30]

Stephen is the product of Pentecost and the classical answer to the prayer of 1 Thessalonians 5:23, "May the God of peace himself sanctify you wholly; and may your spirit and soul and body be kept sound and blameless at the coming of our Lord Jesus Christ." First John 4:16-18 sets forth the same truth in its discussion of perfect love.[31]

5. The church of Pentecost is made orderly so that the divine mission can be accomplished with the greatest degree of effectiveness. Acts gives evidence of (1) orderliness in personal lives, a negative example being that of Ananias and Sapphira, who suffered dramatic divine judgment because of disorder in their own lives—see Acts 5:1-10; (2) orderliness in congregational life, the two major examples being the resolution of the problem regarding the daily distribution of of food to the Hellenistic widows in Acts 6:1-7, and the Council at Jerusalem, "minutes" of which are found in Acts

15: and (3) orderliness in the missionary endeavors of the Church, Acts 1:8 giving the plan of action: "in Jerusalem and in all Judea and Samaria and to the ends of the Earth." This orderly pattern becomes the plan for the Church's expansion as it is set forth in Acts. One is reminded of John Greenleaf Whittier's hymnic words, "Let our ordered lives confess the beauty of thy peace."[32]

6. The Pentecostal effusion breaks down barriers to communication of and participation in the gospel, and builds up that same community of gospel faith. The barriers of language were broken down on the Day of Pentecost (Acts 2:1-12) and the barrier of nationalism was dealt with in Peter's vision prior to the conversion of Cornelius. To the extended family of Cornelius, Peter says, "Truly I perceive that God shows no partiality, but in every nation any one who fears him and does what is right is acceptable to him" (Acts 10:34). But the breaking down of barriers has a divine rationale that extends beyond the mere fact of barriers being destroyed. The ultimate goal is the edification of the community of faith. The two are inextricably bound together in the church of Pentecost: on the one hand, the Spirit's upbuilding of the Church inevitably means the breaking down of barriers to gospel communication and community; and on the other hand, when we are unwilling for the Spirit to break down barriers, the upbuilding of the body of Christ is greatly inhibited. Herman Ridderbos, the Pauline scholar, describes church growth as being both intensive (i.e., development into the fullness of Christ) and extensive (i.e., the spread of the gospel to an increasing number of people.)[33] The edification of the Church is a matter of both spiritual as well as numerical growth. On the one hand, the quality of its extension work is fully related to its growth in Christ, and on the other hand, for the Church to grow in Christ inevitably means that it will be earnestly committed to the missionary mandate of Christ, to go to all peoples. This is the key to understanding Paul's doctrine of gifts. The gifts of the

What the Church Does with Its Eyes

Spirit are manifestations of God's grace in the Church for the singular purpose of building up the whole body of believers into the full stature of Christ, while at the same time building it up numerically as more and more persons are evangelized and brought into mature discipleship.[34]

INSTITUTIONAL STRUCTURES AND THE FELLOWSHIP OF THE SPIRIT

In *The Misunderstanding of the Church*, Emil Brunner develops the thesis that the essential nature of the Church has to do with its personal relatedness to God. In so doing, Brunner is very critical of ecclesiastical structures that, in his view, all too often mitigate against the person-oriented fellowship of the Spirit.[35] He writes,

> The *Ecclesia* of the New Testament, the fellowship of Christian believers, is precisely *not* that which every "church" is at least in part—an institution, a something. The Body of Christ is nothing other than a fellowship of persons. It is "the fellowship of Jesus Christ" (1 Cor. 1:9) or "fellowship of the Holy Ghost" (2 Cor. 13:13; Phil. 2:1) where fellowship or *koinonia* signifies a common participation, a togetherness, a community life. The faithful are bound to each other through their common sharing in Christ and in the Holy Ghost, but that which they have in common is precisely no "thing," no "it," but a "he," Christ and His Holy Spirit.[36]

Whether or not one agrees with Brunner's severe treatment of the Church's institutional structures—and I for one think that he is much too severe—the evidence in Acts does indeed support the conclusion that the true and indispensable mark of the church of Pentecost is the faithful, lively, personal relationship that believers have to Emmanuel ("God with us") and through him to each other. Apart from this faithful, lively, personal relationship, there is no church.

Throughout Old Testament, New Testament, and post-biblical history, the subject of the people of God has been dealt with from two perspectives. The first perspective is that of the sociological, historical, institutional structures that come into existence, develop, divide, unite, die, change, and reproduce. The second perspective is that of the relationally oriented community of faith with which God is well pleased. These, of course, are not mutually exclusive, but neither is it the case that the institutional perspective guarantees the relational, or that the relational is ever possible without the institutional. There are historical examples of both of these (mis)understandings about the connection between the two perspectives. Brunner himself comes very close to the (mis!)-understanding that the two are mutually exclusive when he says that the Church "as the Body of Christ . . . has nothing to do with an organization and has nothing of the character of the institutional about it."[37] The second (mis)understanding of this relationship, namely that the institutional structures guarantee the spiritual reality, is clearly illustrated by the Roman Catholic church with its tradition of clericalism and sacramentalism.

Certainly in the New Testament, the building of churchly, institutional structures is interconnected with the experience of divinely initiated, interpersonal relatedness. While the Pastoral Epistles are the capstone of this interconnectedness, all of the New Testament books, when the whole perspective of each is carefully considered, assume it.[38]

The history of the Church has witnessed many attempts at building institutional structures quite apart from any overtly New Testament type of concern about experiencing the presence and ongoing work of the Holy Spirit.[39] Instead of directing their eyes toward the Emmanuel known to us in the Incarnation and in the Pentecostal effusion, some kind of substitution is made. For instance, the perpetuation of one's own ethnic, cultural, racial, or socio-economic kind might move to center stage. Some examples are the overt establishment of congregations strictly for white factory workers *so that* their special values can be protected, or for German-speaking people *so that* their children will not forget their native tongue, or for American blacks *so that* their black cultural expressions will be maintained, or for upper-class Americans *so that* their degree of sophistication will be protected. The point being made here is not that particular values, languages, and cultural expressions are inconsequential. Rather, the point is that the church that organizes itself primarily for these purposes has made a substitution for Emmanuel and his barrier-breaking work. Whenever the church repents of such substitutions and directs its eyes of faith on Emmanuel, it is the promulgation of the gospel itself that comes to be of utmost importance; it is the perpetuation of the fellowship of reconciliation that gladdens their hearts more than any other endeavor; it is the pursuance of Christ's missionary mandate that becomes the foremost item on the church's agenda. The church that is more interested in telling the world about its own doctrinal distinctives than it is in spreading the gospel needs to avail itself of Pentecost.[40] The church that jealously protects its own kind against the influence of others rather than being open-hearted toward all of God's kind needs to be baptized with the Holy Spirit. The church that is concerned more with the extension of its own institutional structures than it is with the evangelization of the world needs to receive the wind and fire of Pentecost.[41] A young missionary couple of the Church of God (Anderson, Indiana) exude with joy as they tell about attending the services of a large Christian congregation in Seoul, Korea. They write,

> Perhaps the most impressive to us about the service was the obvious importance of prayer. At one point early in the service, the entire congregation joined together to pray aloud for the salvation of Korea. . . . Everyone voiced his or her own prayer aloud during several minutes of intense, fervent praying. It was a moving experience to be joined in prayer to our Father with so many Christians of another land.[42]

They go on to tell about the congregation being led by its pastor to pray for worldwide concerns: "We were especially appreciative of their prayers for the United States and Japan." This congregation prays regularly for the salvation of millions in Japan. It is that kind of missionary commitment that the church in the Book of Acts had; it is that same kind of commitment that the ongoing church of Pentecost continues having.

Institutional structures are both necessary and divinely blessed, providing they give expression to the Spirit of Christ, which is a spirit of redemptive service, a spirit of gospel-oriented missionary work, a spirit of both divine and human sensitivity. But institutional structures can never give expression to the Christly spirit unless the people of God are filled with the Spirit of God.

The effusion of the Holy Spirit gives the Church eyes to see the past fulfilled, the future guaranteed, and the present sanctified in Christ; eyes both to behold the world through the Christly love of God, and to behold the glory of God in the face of Jesus Christ; eyes that rejoice always at the interior work of the Spirit in the lives of believers, but also eyes that look with missionary zeal upon the fields that are white unto harvest.

> Devoted to the study of Scripture
> Expectant in attitude
> Transformed by worship
> Dedicated to service and to social change
> Purified in word, thought, and deed
> Consecrated for missionary endeavor—
>> That is the ongoing church of Pentecost.

Notes

1. A thought-provoking book for worship leaders is Anne Ortlund's *Up with Worship* (Glendale, Calif.: Regal, 1977). "Three Cheers for Stiff, Rigid Rows of Pews! Alternatives may become humanistic" (p. 12)

What the Church Does with Its Eyes

2. See my discussion of Restorationism in Charles W. Carter, ed., *A Contemporary Wesleyan Theology,* 2 vols. (Grand Rapids: Zondervan, 1983). Vol. 1 chapter 1, "Frontiers in Contemporary Theology," section 1, A, 1.

3. For a definitive history of Ecumenical Christianity, see *A History of the Ecumenical Movement*, 2 vols., Ruth Rouse and Stephen Charles Neil, eds., vol. 1 (1517-1948); Harold E. Fey, ed., vol. 2 (1948-1968) (Philadelphia: Westminster Press, 1967, 1970).

4. Typical of the approach designated here as Prophetic Christianity are the writings of Hal Lindsey, *The Late Great Planet Earth* (Grand Rapids: Zondervan, 1970); and *There's a New World Coming: "A Prophetic Odyssey"* (Santa Ana: Vision House, 1973).

5. Two examples of Pacifist Christianity are the interdenominational conference called "New Call to Peacemaking" sponsored by the Church of the Brethren, Friends, and Mennonites (P.O. Box 235, Plainfield, Indiana 46168); and the more broadly representative Fellowship of Reconciliation, Box 271, Nyack, New York 10960.
Two contemporary writers who approach the issues from a distinctively Christian point of view are Ronald J. Sider, *Christ and Violence* (Scottdale: Herald Press, 1979); and John H. Yoder, *Nevertheless: The Varieties and Shortcomings of Religious Pacifism* (Grand Rapids: Eerdmans, 1972).

6. See my discussion of the theology of hope in Carter, *Contemporary Wesleyan Theology*, vol. 1, chapter 1, section 1, A, 3.

7. See Gustavo Gutierrez, *A Theology of Liberation*, translators and eds. Sister Caridad Inda and John Eagleson (Maryknoll: Orbis, 1973). Also, for an example of a severe critique of capitalism written by a North American, see William R. Coats, *God in Public: Political Theology Beyond Niebuhr* (Grand Rapids: Eerdmans, 1974).

8. Some songs originating in the Church of God (Anderson, Indiana) reflect a utopian strain. See *Hymnal of the Church of God* (Anderson: Warner, 1971): no. 453 "The Church's Jubilee" by Charles W. Naylor, stanza 3: "The day of sects and creeds for us

forevermore is past,/Our brotherhood are all the saints upon the world so vast;/We reach our hands in fellowship to every blood-washed one,/While love entwines about each heart in which God's will is done."; no.456 "The Bond of Perfectness" by Daniel S. Warner, stanza 3: " 'God over all and in us all,' and thro' each holy brother;/No power of earth or hell, withal, can rend us from each other."; no. 457 "The Reformation Glory" by Naylor, stanza 4: "Christians all should dwell together in the bonds of peace,/All the clashing of opinions, all the strife should cease."

9. *Ecclesial communities* is a term used in this essay to refer to any type of Christian fellowship that takes institutional form, whether in denominations, movements, hierarchies, brotherhoods, sisterhoods, trans-, non-, or un-denominational organizations. It refers to any kind of institutional form that church life takes.

10. Being "slain in the Spirit" refers to being so overpowered by the "Spirit" that one falls backward and lies in a state of ecstasy for a while. Not all Pentecostalists emphasize this practice, but it is strongly stressed by many of them.

11. Of course, this is by no means a universal practice among Wesleyan/Holiness preachers, but it is a widespread tendency that is naturally congruent with any theology that places such great importance on right living.

12. Matthew 1:23

13. As Jürgen Moltmann says in *Theology of Hope* (New York: Harper & Row, 1967), p. 301, "Christian proclamation shares with the Old Testament tradition its orientation towards the future. Tradition is forward-moving mission into the new situation of the promised future."

14. Contemporary theological reflection about the challenge of being the church is indicated by the following works written from a wide spectrum of Christian tradition. Wesleyan/Holiness Howard A. Snyder, *The Community of the King* (Downers Grove, Ill.: Inter-Varsity Press, 1978); Roman Catholic Karl Rahner, *The Shape of the Church to Come* (New York: Seabury, 1974); Reformed G. C. Berhouwer, *The Church*, James E. Davison, trans. (Grand Rapids: Eerdmans, 1976); Pentecostal Melvin L.

Hodges, *A Theology of the Church and Its Mission* (Springfield: Gospel Publishing House, 1977); theologian of hope Jürgen Moltmann, *The Church in the Power of the Spirit*, Margaret Kohl, trans.(New York: Harper & Row, 1977).

15. For a concise history of nineteenth-century unity movements in the United States see Rouse and Neill, eds. *History of Ecumenical Movement*, vol. 1, chapters 5 and 6. A standard introduction to twentieth-century developments is Samuel McCrea Cavert, *On the Road to Christian Unity* (Westport: Greenwood, 1979). An extensive study of a twentieth-century church that began as a nineteenth-century unity movement is John W. V. Smith, *The Quest for Holiness and Unity* (Anderson, Ind.: Warner Press, 1980).

16. United Methodist Bishop Emerson S. Colaw of Minnesota has suggested four approaches to dealing with the decline of membership in the so-called mainline churches in the United States: Emphasize hope, community, ethnics, and the Holy Spirit. See "Suggestions on Ending Mainline Church Decline," *Christianity Today*, vol. 27, no. 2 (January 21, 1983), 30 ff. Colaw is quoted as having said, "The Spirit is the spirit of surprise. We don't know when or where God will renew the church, but we do believe it will happen."

17. N. A. Nissiotis, "Interpreting Orthodoxy," *Ecumenical Review*, no. 14 (1961), 26: "Orthodoxia means the wholeness of the people sharing the right conviction concerning the Event of God in Christ and His Church and the right expression of this faith."

18. John Calvin's dictum reads, "Wherever we find the word of God purely preached and heard, and the sacraments administered according to the institution of Christ, there, it is not to be doubted, is a Church of God." *Institutes of the Christian Religion*, John Allen, trans., 2 vols. (Philadelphia: Presbyterian Board of Christian Education, 1936), 2:281 (*Institutes* 4. 1. 9).

19. Lycurgus M. Starkey, Jr., *The Work of the Holy Spirit* (New York: Abingdon Press, 1962), 150.

20. J. Robert Nelson, *Criterion for the Church* (New York:

Abingdon Press, 1962), 15.

21. William Barclay, *The Promise of the Spirit* (Philadelphia: Westminster Press, 1960), 57.

22. All biblical references are from the Revised Standard Version.

23. Clark Pinnock, "Opening the Church to the Charismatic Dimension," *Christianity Today*, vol. 25, no. 11 (June 12, 1981), p. 16 [785]. Pinnock is not using *charismatic* as a synonym for *glossolalia*.

24. Pinnock, p. 16.

25. W. T. Conner, *The Work of the Holy Spirit* (Nashville: Broadman, 1940), 57ff.

26. Helpful discussions may be found in Barclay, *Promise of the Spirit*, chapters 4 and 6; Charles W. Carter, *The Person and Ministry of the Holy Spirit: A Wesleyan Perspective* (Grand Rapids: Baker, 1977), chapters 6-10; Conner, *Work of the Holy Spirit*, chapter 4; James D. G. Dunn, *Jesus and the Spirit* (Philadelphia: Westminster Press, 1975), chapter 6; Dale Moody, *Spirit of the Living God* (Nashville: Broadman, 1976), chapter 3; Paul D. Opsahl, ed., *The Holy Spirit in the Life of the Church* (Minneapolis: Augsburg, 1978), pp. 28-38; and R. A. Torrey, *The Person and Work of the Holy Spirit* (Grand Rapids: Zondervan, 1974), chapters 20-23.

27. See Oscar Cullmann and F. J. Leenhardt, *Essays on the Lord's Supper*, J. G. Davies, trans. (Atlanta: John Knox, 1958).

28. See Acts 2:42-47 for Luke's summary statement about this new fellowship in Christ. Also, see J. Robert Nelson's development of the implications of this passage in his *Criterion for the Church*.

29. Robert E. Coleman, *The Songs of Heaven* (Old Tappan, N. J.: Revell, 1980), 67.

30. First Corinthians 16:22, "If any one has no love for the Lord, let him be accursed. Our Lord, come!" The Aramaic term used in the Greek text is *Maranatha*. The idea is that the one who

loves the Lord wholeheartedly has no fear of the Lord's return, and consequently joins in praying what Ralph Martin calls "the oldest prayer of which we have record" (p. 32) in his *Worship in the Early Church* (Grand Rapids: Eerdmans, 1976); also, pp. 128, 131.

31. Second Peter 3:11-14 is a passage that stresses the believer's responsibility in the establishment of absolute devotion to Christ, regardless of the trials of life. See my discussion in John E Hartley and R. Larry Shelton, eds., *An Inquiry into Soteriology from a Biblical Theological Perspective* (Anderson, Ind.: Warner, 1981), chapter titled "Salvation in the General Epistles," especially p. 212ff.

32. John Greenleaf Whittier, "Dear Lord and Father of Mankind," stanza 3.

33. Herman Ridderbos, *Paul: An Outline of His Theology*, John Richard DeWitt, trans. (Grand Rapids: Eerdmans, 1975), 432-38. "One could speak of the enlargement and preservation, of the extensive-missionary and the intensive-confirmatory element of this upbuilding, which in the work of God are one" (p. 433).

34. The subject of divine gifts as viewed in the whole of Scripture is carefully developed in John Koenig, *Charismata: God's Gifts for God's People* (Philadelphia: Westminster, 1978). Also see Arlo F. Newell, *Receive the Holy Spirit* (Anderson, Ind.: Warner Press, 1978), chapter 10, "Charismata: The Gifts of the Spirit."

35. Emil Brunner, *The Misunderstanding of the Church,* Harold Knight, trans. (Philadelphia: Westminster Press, 1953), especially pp. 116ff. "Clerical parsonic ecclesiasticism has ever been the greatest enemy of the Christian message and of brotherhood rooted in Christ" (p. 117).

36. Brunner, p. 117.

37. Brunner, p. 117. This position is also suggestive of the radical view held by D. S. Warner, leader of a nineteenth-century unity-holiness movement, who encouraged Christians to flee from the "Babylonian Captivity" of denominational structures. For an analysis of Warner's ecclesiology, see my "Experiential Salvation and Christian Unity in the Thought of Seven Theologians of the

Church of God (Anderson, Indiana)" (unpublished Th.D. dissertation, Boston University School of Theology, 1973), pp. 64-90. In one particularly pointed article, Warner writes, "Surely the holiness people are in perils in sectism, and in perils of comeoutism. In perils in old antiholiness sects, and in still greater perils in 'new holiness sects.' What shall they do? Behold them rebounding from ism to ism. . . . Poor fellows, where shall they flee? Well we lift up our voice like a trumpet, and sound an alarm on all God's mountain, saying 'escape for your life,' tarry not in Sodom, nor in all the plain of babylon. Flee far out of all isms. . . . Get under the blood . . . and abide in Christ alone, and you shall find rest for your souls." (D. S. Warner, "Propping up the Walls, or Banner Deceptions," *The Gospel Trumpet*, vol. 6, no. 19 [December 1, 1884], 1).

38. Major consideration is given to this subject in the writings of Eduard Schweizer, *Church Order in the New Testament*, Frank Clarke, trans. (Naperville: Alec R. Allenson, 1961). Also, *The Church as the Body of Christ* (Richmond: John Knox, 1964.) Also, Ferdinand Hahn, August Strobel, and Eduard Schweizer, *The Beginnings of the Church in the New Testament,* Iain and Ute Nicol, trans. (Minneapolis: Augsburg, 1970).

39. A helpful analysis of the historical and sociological factors influencing the history of American Protestantism is Martin E. Marty, *Righteous Empire: The Protestant Experience in America (New York: Dial, 1970).* Also, *The Public Church: Mainline-Evangelical-Catholic* (New York: Crossroad, 1981).

40. For a very direct confrontation with this issue see "The Sectarian Spirit," *Verdict*, vol. 4, no. 3 (March 1981). For further discussion of the *Verdict* articles, see *Centering on Ministry*, vol. 7, no. 2 (Spring, 1982) published by the Center for Pastoral Studies, Anderson, Indiana. Articles include James Earl Massey, "The Church: A Community," Barry L. Callen, "When a Movement Ceases to Move," and my "Christianity—In a Sectarian Mold or in a Wholistic One?"

41. See Carl E. Braaten, *The Flaming Center: A Theology of the Christian Mission* (Philadelphia: Fortress, 1977); Lesslie Newbigin, *The Open Secret: Sketches for a Missionary Theology*

What the Church Does with Its Eyes

(Grand Rapids: Eerdmans, 1978); J. Verkuyl, *Contemporary Missiology: An Introduction*, Dale Cooper, trans. and ed. (Grand Rapids: Eerdmans, 1978); and C. Peter Wagner (Chairperson of The Strategy Working Committee), *To Reach the Unreached: A Report to the Lausanne Committee for World Evangelization* (Monrovia: World Vision, MARC, 1978).

42. Cheryl and Bernard Barton, letter distributed by Park Place Church of God, Anderson, Indiana, January 1983.

Gilbert W. Stafford

Unity and Division in the American Holiness Movement
John W. V. Smith

Of all the theological issues related, either directly or indirectly, to the American holiness movement in the years preceding and following the turn of the twentieth century, the most troublesome was the "church question." In using this term the holiness adherents did not mean they were engaged in a serious quest for a biblical ecclesiology; they were referring to the practical matter of how best to promote the holiness teaching that they regarded as being so central to vital Christian faith and experience. As the movement gained momentum the crucial question with which they were forced to deal was whether it was in the best interest of the furtherance of holiness doctrine to promote it within existing denominations or to allow and encourage the formation of a new group or groups with this teaching as a central focus. In wrestling with this question, beginning around 1880, the American holiness movement entered into almost four hectic decades of debate, discord, and division—intermingled with concomitant developments toward reconciliation, reinforcement, and realignment. Even though by 1920 present patterns of structure in the holiness movement were basically established, the same issues have persisted, though the processes for dealing with them have become less volatile and more regularized. The problems of independency, come-outism, put-outism, no-churchism, regionalism, localism, and associationalism were and are all part of this difficult church question.

In order to understand more adequately the internal dynamics of this movement in which such vigorous interaction of strong cohesive and divisive factors have prevailed, a series of generalizations will be posited and examined. Using a basically historical framework for analysis, with concomitant theological issues and practical implications dealt with in context, the history of the American holiness movement will be reviewed with a focus on the issues of unity and division both within the movement itself and as it has related to the whole Christian witness.

.1. *Holiness teaching and the holiness movement have been fundamentally and intentionally transdenominational.*

The fact is easily documented that the central leaders of the holiness movement never intended that the proponents of this doctrine should be confined to a single denomination. Although most of these leaders were Methodists, their vision of the field for the promotion of this work was a broad as the Christian faith itself. The official "call" to that first organizational camp meeting in Vineland, New Jersey, in 1867 makes the interdenominational emphasis doubly clear. Alfred Cookman phrased it well:

> We affectionately invite all, irrespective of denominational ties, interested in the subject of the higher Christian life, to come together and spend a week in God's great temple of nature. . . . Come, brothers and sisters of the various denominations, and let us, in this forest-meeting, as in other meetings for the promotion of holiness, furnish an illustration of evangelical union, and make common supplication for the descent of the Spirit upon ourselves, the church, the nation, and the world.[1]

Unity and Division

The response at the meeting itself was a vindication of the inclusiveness of the call. In reporting this ten-day encampment in the *Guide to Holiness*, G. Hughes lifts up some of the highlights of the first national holiness camp meeting. Among other observations he notes the following:

> Another striking feature of the meeting was the fact that so many Christian denominations were represented. Presbyterians, Baptists, Episcopalians, Lutherans, Friends, and Methodists were all dwelling together in sweetest harmony. Never was there a more beautiful illustration of the Psalmist's declaration,—"Behold how good and how pleasant it is for brethren to dwell together in unity! " One Presbyterian minister had come from Illinois to receive the baptism of fire; and he did receive it. A Baptist minister from Philadelphia came for the holy anointing, and the Spirit of power came upon him. He went to the Baptist church in Vineland on Sabbath morning, and preached to them on the text, "And the very God of peace sanctify you wholly," and held up to them distinctly the privilege of full salvation in the blood of the Lamb.[2]

In reporting the following year's camp meeting at Manheim, Pennsylvania, which attracted a reported 25,000 people, one supporter noted the wide representation from many different groups and claimed a fraternal spirit so prevailed that he "was utterly unable to distinguish . . . one denomination from another."[3]

In order to preserve this transdenominational character of the holiness movement the national association and the various regional associations that were later formed stipulated that "constituent members shall be persons . . . who are members in good standing in some evangelical church."[4]

The idea of isolating the doctrine as the sole property of any group was strongly resisted. Vigorous enthusiasm was experienced in the identification of holiness people, holiness associations, holiness bands, holiness camp meetings, revivals, conferences, and conventions, but resistance was strong against the designation of any group as a holiness church.

Even greater abhorrence was indicated toward the threat of forming new denominations or sects under the holiness banner. In 1880, for instance, M. L. Haney, a prominent leader in the Western Holiness Association, in a convention at Jacksonville, Illinois, warned against those who "have desired and advocated the organization of a distinctively *Holiness* church," declaring that the holiness movement had always been "designed of God to spread scriptural holiness in existing churches, and thus fit them to subjugate the world for Christ."[5]

Because of this deliberate transdenominational stance, no advice was given to holiness converts about church membership. Each made his or her own decision, and each was charged to be a promoter of holiness in his or her own denomination. It was understood, however, that one's commitment to holiness should supersede other loyalties. C. J. Fowler, long-time president of the National Holiness Association, warned in 1908, "A great danger is . . . that real holiness will be wasted or weakened in losing sight of a genuine catholicity, in one's zeal for some local or denominational interest."[6] Much earlier, in 1880, another advocate, Daniel S. Warner, had affirmed that this "conglomeration of sects" in the holiness movement only proved its "divinity." Only the "all resolvent and utilizing virtues of holiness" could join "into such loving band of union . . . elements from the various disintegrated and selfish parties of Israel."[7]

Even though the strong stand against independency and separation on the part of the major leaders was not able to stem the tide of schism, in the late nineteenth and early twentieth centuries the National Holiness Association continued to speak out against "come-outism," to encourage adherents to become a leavening influence in their own denominations, and later to provide a vehicle for cooperation among the various new holiness bodies that the movement had spawned.[8] All the later developments continue to emphasize the interdenominational character of the movement.

Unity and Division

The focus of attention has been on promotion of the doctrine and practice of holiness and not on other affiliations that a person might have. Wide and diverse participation in all the associations was eagerly sought after because this broadened the potential field for promotion. Although holiness as a doctrine has been developed and advanced most specifically by those in the Arminian-Wesleyan tradition, it never has been regarded by its proponents as private property of the Methodists. The teaching has been presented as biblical and Christian and available to all, regardless of their denomination.

2. *Specific emphasis on the doctrine of holiness has tended to foster disunity.*

Certainly nothing is inherent in the doctrine of holiness that would lead to separateness or division among Christians. On the theoretical face of it, quite the opposite would be true. Such terms as *perfect love, Christian perfection, sanctification,* and so forth suggest anything but dissension and disunity. The fact of the matter is, as any student of the holiness movement knows well, holiness has been the occasion for a considerable amount of bitter debate and many severed relationships. The "saints" not only have fought their adversaries, but also have battled one another. Even in an era in which harsh polemics were in style, they often exhibited a pungent vocabulary of notable causticity and graphic castigation. Their deep commitment to the doctrine and their intense fervor in propagating it made holiness people not only strong protagonists but also formidable adversaries.

The potential divisiveness of holiness teaching was recognized quite early in the movement's history. Jessie T. Peck, a holiness advocate who was later to become a Methodist bishop, wrote in 1858 that he feared schism might follow efforts at organized holiness promotion within the church. He warned that it might lead to "invidious distinctions, . . .

jealousies, heart-burnings and divisions," even though these would not be intended by holiness organizers. He enjoined the holiness brethren to "permeate the entire church," not to become a faction within it.[9]

Despite Peck's advice, his fears of schism soon began to be realized. Holiness separateness seems to have developed first within the parent body itself, Methodism. Even though the holiness emphasis took on and encouraged the transdenominational character already described, it began as, and until the 1890s continued to be, a movement to reform the Methodist church.[10] In the face of a rapidly changing church and culture the major leaders saw their primary mission as restoring and preserving old-time Methodism. But holiness teaching was not universally accepted in Methodism. Despite the fact that perfectionism was rooted in Wesleyan theology and was espoused by many influential Methodist leaders, the attack procedures of the advocates of holiness produced a climate of encounter and tension. The associations, the conferences, and the numerous holiness periodicals were mostly unsanctioned by and consequently uncontrolled by the Methodist church. As free-ranging evangelists sought access to every community, whether invited or not, they placed all opposing voices, including the majority of Methodist pastors, under judgment—a position that inevitably produced conflict and eventually separation.

A second contributing factor to divisiveness was the development of the regional holiness associations and the local holiness bands. These loosely developed structures were eventually to become the fountainhead of independency—an alternative to unsympathetic local churches or denominations. Starting in Illinois with the Western Holiness Association in 1872, at least a half dozen other regional associations sprang up in the next decade. Two of these, the Southwestern and the Texas Associations, actually became the foundation of new denominations, and all of them, with the possible exception of the Iowa Association, were open to the

Unity and Division

advocates of independency. At the 1880 meeting of the Western Association in Jacksonville, Illinois, for instance, two of the speakers emphasized that holiness outranked the church in the Christian's list of priorities. J. W. Caughlan, a Missouri Methodist, after noting that holiness work had prospered only where regular holiness bands had been organized, continued, "In places where out of regard to ecclesiastical influences, such organization has been omitted, the holiness work has come to nought. *Those who work for Christ have to consecrate the church,* and go forward.[11] Thomas K. Doty, a Wesleyan Connection minister from Cleveland, sounded an even stronger note as he urged his hearers to "bring everything in your church work to bear on the work of holiness. While you do this you must be saved from the church.[12]

In May 1885, B. A. Washburn of the Southern California and Arizona Holiness Association wrote a special letter to the first General Holiness Assembly convening in Chicago in which he detailed ten reasons for sanctioning the formation of independent holiness bodies. Even though the General Assembly's chairperson, George Hughes, barred the letter from consideration, the fact that it was sent indicates a rising voice toward independency in the regional associations.[13]

The most specific manifestation of divisiveness fostered by the holiness emphasis was the separation of factions and the formation of new denominations. Although few groups would admit to intentional divisiveness, the fact remains that almost without exception the holiness bodies came into being through schismatic action on the part of those who were vigorously upholding the doctrine in the face of opposition in the parent body. The general procedure is well illustrated in the Declaration of Principles adopted by the General Holiness Assembly of 1885:

> Professors of holiness should not voluntarily surrender their Church privileges for trivial causes. But, if an oppressive hand be laid upon them in any case by Church authority,

solely for professing holiness, or for being identified with the cause of Holiness, depriving them of the privileges of Christian communion, they should then adjust themselves to circumstances, as may be required in order to have the continued enjoyment of the ordinances of our holy religion.[14]

Such separations, of course, were always justified as the result of the "hard core of resistance" in the parent group rather than any lack of wisdom or charitableness on the part of the sanctified rebels. William M. Greathouse well describes the oft-repeated process:

Increasingly, the people who had espoused the doctrine, which was never meant to be a "theological provincialism," found themselves unwelcome in their parent denominations. With agapeic hesitancy, but with New Testament poignancy, they formed small denominations.[15]

In reviewing the formation of this multitude of independent churches in the wake of the holiness revival, Timothy L. Smith, in an excellent chapter titled "The Church Question, 1880-1900," analyzes the complex of factors that produced this circumstance. He notes first that the holiness emphasis found adherents among people from a wide variety of backgrounds, both religiously and culturally, so that the movement itself was far from being homogeneous in character. Very early there emerged a basic cleavage between the rural and urban wings of the awakening, the former being more emotional and rigid in defining standards and the latter being more intellectual and flexible.

Smith then isolates four factors that individually and collectively contributed to the fragmentizing and "sectizing" of the holiness emphasis in America:

(1) the persistent opposition of ecclesiastical officials to independent holiness associations and publishing agencies; (2) the recurrent outburst of fanaticism among persons who were members of the associations but not of the churches; (3) the outbreak in the 1890s of strenuous attacks upon the doctrine of sanctification itself; and (4) the increasing activity of urban holiness preachers in city mission and social work.[16]

Unity and Division

The story of the formation of these many holiness denominations is sufficiently well known that it need not be
detailed here. One writer has estimated that as many as one
hundred separate groups were brought into existence by the
divisive activity of the proponents of holiness.[17] Even though
documentation of this figure might be difficult, one really
cannot deny that holiness preaching and teaching have
contributed significantly to the divided state of the Church.

3. *Holiness leaders generally have tended to give only
marginal attention to Christian unity and have steadfastly
defended the denominational system.*

The fact that holiness people have been strongly associational does not mean they have been concerned about
Christian unity. Their cooperation has been focused on a
specific purpose—the promotion of holiness—and has not
been directed toward the overcoming of division and the
unification of the Church. One might go even further and
state that the central emphasis on personal holiness has so
occupied the thought of leaders of the movement that little
attention has been given even to articulating a doctrine of
the Church, and much less to formulating concepts of the
unity of the Church. This is not to say that a concern for the
nature of the Church and its unity is entirely absent, for
some significant formulations have been made, but one can
examine a whole section of books on holiness in a seminary
library and find very few of them that include any treatment
of the ecclesiastical implications of the doctrine.

The deep concern on the part of early leaders of the
movement that the holiness emphasis not be confined to a
single religious group put them in the position of condon-
ing—and seeking to work within—all existing groups. A
holiness preacher was not just a holiness preacher; he was a
Methodist, Baptist, or Presbyterian preacher who preached
holiness. As the associations were formed, the usual specific
stipulation that participants were to be "members in good

standing" of some Christian denomination was tantamount to putting a blessing on the existing system.

Even after the fragmentation process began, a strong attachment was still felt to the importance of denominational affiliation. The call to the 1901 Chicago Assembly contains the statement, "Persons will be enrolled as members who bring certificates from some branch of the evangelical Church, or from organizations that maintain a fraternal spirit and attitude toward the Church."[18] In the Salutation this principle is explicated further in regard to persons who, because of their fidelity to the cause of holiness, may have been expelled from their churches:

> They should be regarded with charity, treated with tenderness and consideration, and not disfellowshiped by the holiness brethren or branded with epithets of an unpleasant and reproachful character. Our advice to such would be in all cases to seek affiliation as early as possible with some organized body of Christian people who believe in and are committed to the holiness work.[19]

In order to avoid a position that seemed to put a blessing on division in the Church, one writer found comfort in drawing a distinction between *denomination* and *sect*. The sect, says Joseph H. Smith, is a "child of carnality" while the denomination is sometimes a "child of providence." He regarded the latter as necessary to meet the diversities of "localities, languages, governmental restrictions, ancestral heritages, etc." incident to the worldwide propagation of Christianity. "As there were twelve tribes, but *one Israel*, so the body has various members, but one life within all; and different 'branches' of the church may all yet be as of one Vine."[20] At other points Smith utilizes Calvin's "visible-invisible" rationale for denominational divisions in the Church.[21]

In spite of widespread accusation to the contrary, holiness leaders, almost with one voice, denounced "come-outism." Even the come-outers denounced it, except they put the onus on the other parties and accused them of "crush-outism."[22] Regardless of the rhetoric, it is evident that the proponents of holiness had high regard for existing denominations, were reluctant to withdraw from them unless circumstances became intolerable, and in forming new denominations they simply took advantage of the system and did little to try to change its nature.[23]

4. *Holiness groups have tended to be aloof from general ecumenical activity.*

The massive ecumenical bustle of the twentieth century developed largely without either the encouragement or the assistance of holiness-oriented leadership. Currently no avowedly holiness body in the United States is a full member of the World Council of Churches. One, the Salvation Army, has held membership. The British Salvation Army, however, does participate in the World Council. The National Council of Churches lists no holiness churches in its membership, but five holiness groups and one Canadian body with holiness orientation have been approved for participation in selected units of the council's programmatic activity. The degree and extent of participation would vary widely from group to group and from time to time.

The ecumenical picture of holiness denominations involved with the National Association of Evangelicals is considerably different. Here a high degree of participation is clearly evident. Of the twelve member bodies of the Christian Holiness Association, seven of them are also members of NAE; and of the six organizations listed as "cooperating" with the CHA, two are members of the NAE. The sum total adds up to the fact that half of these holiness groups are affiliated with NAE. It is notable, however, that some of the larger bodies—such as the Church of the Nazarene, the Salvation Army, and the Church of God (Anderson, Indiana)—are among the other half who do not cooperate. To these must be added a significant number of holiness groups that do not even have a relationship with the CHA.[24]

If one were to attempt to analyze the reasons for this basically nonecumenical stance, one would find difficulty in formulating any overall generalizations. From our review thus far, however, at least one fact is historically evident. Almost without exception the holiness groups were born out of conflict with the very denominations that make up the mainline ecumenical organizations, thus creating an inherent, though often unconscious, reluctance to lock arms with one's former adversaries. Beyond this are the usual evangelical objections to cooperating with groups more "liberal" in theology and more "leftist" in politics. Pronouncements on social issues and involvement in protest activism have not been highly regarded by holiness people as proper procedures for proclamation, albeit there is evidence of a heightening social concern among all evangelicals.

These theological and social issues would not apply, of course, to noncooperation through the NAE. Here the reasons for aloofness would be less accusative and probably less specific. For some it is simply, "We have plenty to do and we're making it well on our own." For others there are problems of attitude and spirit. Still others see all conciliarism as an abortive approach to true Christian unity, and so they do not join any organization for this purpose.

Putting it all together, one must conclude that holiness people have not been highly enthusiastic about the promotion of unity through entering into associational relationships with a broad spectrum of other Christians through the nation or around the world.

5. *Some holiness leaders have looked to "perfect love" as the only escape from division in the Church, and have envisioned a visible fellowship of all the "saints."*

In his introduction to the report of the 1901 General Holiness Assembly, S. B. Shaw observes that "many hearts have been greatly burdened and have been crying to God for union among all of God's children, especially among all those that believe in holiness of heart as possible through faith in the cleansing blood of Christ and by the baptism of the Holy Ghost."[25] Earlier (1896) holiness evangelist L. L. Pickett had declared, "Remember, when you people are lamenting the lack of unity among the people of God, that the remedy is to be found in sanctification. It is the doctrine of oneness among the children of God."[26]

Even earlier a number of other advocates of holiness had suggested that an obvious implication of the sanctifying experience should be the removing of barriers that divide Christians from one another. In his 1858 holiness classic, *The Central Idea of Christianity*, Methodist Jesse T. Peck, following his warning against schism because of holiness promotion, stoutly affirmed that "strong and indissoluble Christian union" should "be the result of increased attention to the doctrine of holiness."[27] Another early expression of this viewpoint is found in a letter to the *Guide to Holiness* in 1867 from Southern Methodist Bishop John Wilkins. He raises the question as to whether "the element of 'Perfect Love' is of sufficient power in the various branches of Methodism to leaven the *animus* of the whole denomination with such Christly love as that we shall hear no longer of that bitter hate between Northern and Southern Methodism." He goes ahead to state that he does not feel that the time is ripe for reuniting the two churches, but there is need, he says, "to remove the fretting friction." He continues by affirming, "There is enough of 'Perfect Love' in both branches to accomplish the desired result."[26] Admittedly, considerable difference exists between bringing peace to Methodism and healing the breaches in all Christendom, but the suggested remedy could well apply in both cases, for the malady is the same.

In the 1873 National Holiness Camp Meeting at Landesville, Pennsylvania, Edgar M. Levy, a long-time Baptist participant in the movement, observed that all previous efforts to achieve Christian unity have been thwarted because of, as Dieter puts it, the "impossibility of creating *uniformity* in the expression of belief in the constitution of the church, and in the administration of the ordinances." But as Levy himself went on to say,

> at last we have discovered the basis for Christian unity. The sanctification of the believers of every name, create unity in the great Christian brotherhood, such as no creed has ever been able to accomplish. Here . . . we have . . . an exhibition of Christian unity as thrills one's soul to behold. A unity not in ordinances; a unity not in church government; a unity not in forms of worship; a unity not in mere letter of creed—but in . . . the baptism of the Holy Spirit. As it is the nature of sin to separate, disintegrate, and repel, *it is the nature of holiness to unite and adjust and harmonize.*[29]

Thomas K. Doty, in the 1880 Western Union Holiness Convention at Jacksonville, Illinois, stated that he did not "believe in this denominational idea as God's idea. He permits it, and so must we." He then continued,

> We must work to bring about what Jesus prayed for—"that they all may be one." The time will come when these denominations will crumble; and the sooner the better, if we can build on a firmer basis. . . . Let us . . . lay aside our denominational jackets, and go to work together as the servants of our Lord Jesus Christ. The body of Christ is one.[30]

Other expressions suggesting holiness as the hope for unity have appeared from time to time in the literature of the movement, but the most articulate exponent of sanctification as the remedy for division was Daniel S. Warner, an Ohio preacher of the (Winebrennerian) Churches of God. He was led to accept the holiness teaching and experience in about 1877 and become an ardent promoter of the doctrine. In 1878 he was expelled from his denomination for noncooperation and failure to abide by admonitions given him by the eldership regarding his activities as a traveling evangelist.

Unity and Division

He was accused of creating agitation in particular congregations by his vigorous preaching of holiness. Shortly after his expulsion he entered the following note in his diary:

> The Lord showed me that holiness could never prosper upon sectarian soil encumbered by human creeds and party names, and he gave me a new commission to join holiness and all truth together and build up the apostolic church of the living God. Praise his name! I will obey him.[31]

During the following several months Warner's thoughts concerning the relationship between holiness and unity began to take shape. He launched into the preparation of a manuscript that was published in 1880 by the Evangelical United Mennonite Publishing Society under the title of *Bible Proofs of the Second Work of Grace.* In order to understand adequately his views, a rather extended series of quotations from this work will be noted.

To begin with, he clearly regarded all divisions in the Church as sinful:

> Oft the enlightened Christian's conscience inquires whether it is right for the Church to be divided thus, into a plurality of sects or denominations, with their respective human creeds and party names. In the light of truth, we are compelled to answer, No. And for the simple reason that these parties are not of Divine origin. Christ is the source of all true union among His disciples, and all divisions between them and the world; while the Devil is the instigation of all divisions in the Church, and all union between it and the world.[32]

Again:

> It is a solemn fact that adherence in different denominations is the Devil's wedge, whereby the unity of the Spirit, so perfectly procured in the grace of perfect love, is again destroyed. Party names, party creeds, and party spirits, almost of necessity go together; and the natural return of this spirit, because of membership in a fragmentary Church, takes more souls off of God's altar than everything else together.[33]

This party feeling, which he describes as "very sin," not only destroys brotherly love among Christians; it also hinders the work of evangelization. "The division of the Church into parties not only destroys the power and holiness thereof, but is the greatest impediment to the conversion of the world to God."[34] He mourns this dire result of division among Christians:

> O, the thousands of souls, that are being lost to all eternity through the selfish, wicked and carnal spirit of our churchism! God is dishonored, yea, robbed of the purchase of His Son's death, and infidelity stalks abroad; the result of a divided house.[35]

> Can it be said of professors of holiness that they have "one heart" and "one mind" while some have a mind to be Presbyterian, others Baptist, others United Brethren, and others have a mind to adhere to the several different sects of Methodism? Have they "one heart and one way," when they rise from the solemn altar in the holiness meeting and go, each one in his own way, to the synagogue of *his own sect*?[36]

For Warner, neither the problem nor its solution is of a corporate nature:

> I would lay the responsibility of this enormous evil just where God places it, and all other sin. We will not be judged by sects, states, nor even by neighborhoods and towns, but "every *one* shall give an account of *himself* to God."
>
> A revival of holiness in a community is the result of personal consecration and faith; and its relapse will be in proportion to the number of individuals that remove the sacrifice from the altar. There is no such thing as thorough holiness, except as wrought by the Sanctifier in individual hearts; and if, as has been said, and as I verily believe, thorough and widespread holiness destroys denominations—burns up sectarian distinctions—it must do it in your heart, as an individual.[37]

To accomplish this desired end—to destroy denominationalism and achieve Christian unity—requires action on the part of sanctified persons. Though Warner denied the charge of "come-outism," affirming that urging people to come out of one sect into another was furthest from his thought, he nevertheless left little doubt regarding what he felt a sanctified Christian should do.

> If you are a true, intelligent Bible Christian, a holy, God fearing man, you must cast off every human yoke, withdraw fellowship from, and renounce every schismatic and humanly constituted party in the professed body of Christ. Instead of belonging to "some branch," you will simply belong to Christ, and be a branch yourself in Him, the "true vine." Instead of remaining identified with any sect—i.e., cut-off party, "directly or indirectly the results of sin"—you will claim membership in, and fellowship with the "one and indivisible Church, that God has on earth, and which is made up of all, and singularly who are born of the Spirit." On this broad and divinely established platform, and here only, can you stand clear of the sin of sectarianism and the blood of immortal souls that perish through its pernicious influence.[38]

In Warner's mind the views he expressed were not to be identified with the "no-churchism" propounded by John P. Brooks and others in the holiness movement. He declared,

> I am not advocating the no-church theory, that we hear of in the west, but the one holy Church of the Bible, not bound together by rigid articles of faith, but perfectly united in love, under the primitive glory of the Sanctifier, "continuing steadfastly in the Apostles' doctrine and fellowship," and taking captive the world for Jesus.[39]

In summarizing his views Warner lists five conclusions:

> From what has been said, and the uniform teaching of the Bible, the following facts are very evident:
> 1. The division of the Church into sects is one of Satan's most effectual, if not the very greatest means of destroying human souls.
> 2. Its enormous sin must be answered for by individual adherents to, and supporters of, sects.
> 3. The only remedy for this dreadful plague, is thorough

sanctification, and this is only wrought by a personal, individual contact with the blood of Christ through faith.

4. The union required by the Word of God is both a spiritual and visible union.

5. The divisions of the Church are caused by elements that are foreign to it as a divinely constituted body, by deposits of the enemy, which exist in the hearts and practices of individual members, involving their responsibility and requiring their personal purgation.[40]

And finally, he affirms his conviction that neither holiness nor unity can progress unless they do it together.

It is, indeed, my honest conviction that the great holiness reform cannot go forward with the sweeping power and permanent triumph that God designs it should, until the Gospel be so preached, and consecration become so thorough, that the blood of Christ may reach, and wash away every vestige of denomination distinction, and *"perfect into one"*—yea, *one* indeed and in truth—all the santified.[41]

Even though Warner held these convictions strongly, he did not take any hasty action. In the summer of 1880 he played a very active role in the Jacksonville, Illinois, holiness assembly, making one of the presentations and serving on a committee. The following year at Terre Haute, Indiana, however, he withdrew from the association because the assembly refused to remove what he called the "sect endorsing clause" from their bylaws. He felt that the requirement that a participant in the association must be a member of some church, was approval of the sinful system. In October of that same year he withdrew from the Northern Indiana Eldership of the Church of God (a small holiness group with which he had affiliated three years earlier) and took his stand "with Christ alone." From this action—and similar steps taken shortly thereafter in Michigan and Ohio—a nondenominational holiness movement emerged that is known as the Church of God (Anderson, Indiana).

So—there have been and still are those who hold the view that true holiness destroys division and produces genuine Christian unity.

Unity and Division

6. *Adherents of holiness have evidenced a basically cooperative stance toward each other through associational structures and significant denominational mergers.*

Donald W. Dayton has observed that "although denominations within the holiness movement consistently ignore the conciliar movements on the national and international level, they are fiercely ecumenical within their own circle."[42] The tendencies toward divisiveness and aloofness mentioned earlier have not subverted an even stronger inclination to devise ways to identify with and establish vehicles of cooperation with others of like mind and spirit.

Holiness people have never been loners. From the "class meetings" of the Wesleys to the "Tuesday meetings" of the Palmers to the "camp meetings" of modern times, togetherness has been integral to the holiness emphasis. This togetherness has never been incidental or casual; it has been deliberate and planned. From the earliest days of the movement the proponents of this doctrine have joined together in transdenominational associations, assemblies, and bands. The early associations, however, including what came to be the National Holiness Association, were not coalescent of groups but of individuals. These structures were conceived as completely nonecclesiastical. Their function was solely for the promotion of holiness, and no participant's denominational affiliation or loyalty was challenged. The prevailing attitude on this point is well expressed in a resolution passed by the 1901 General Holiness Assembly held in Chicago:

> To more effectively promote the spread of holiness, and unify our work, we recommend the organization of bands and county and state associations, with a uniformity of constitution and by-laws. That this Assembly, composed of members from at least twenty different evangelical churches, declare that these bands and associations are in no sense churches, were never intended to be churches, and are not to take the place of churches, but are simply a union of people for the promotion and conservation of holiness.[43]

At various times throughout the history of the movement some have sought to unify the whole effort through some central coordinating agency. S. B. Shaw, of Lansing, Michigan, for example, had a dream of forming a national holiness union and was one of the promoters of the assemblies held in Chicago first in 1885 and again in 1901. He hoped that these assemblies would eventuate in just such a union, but it never developed that way. The association approach yielded to the drive toward separate denominations. Before the 1901 meeting, Shaw himself had led a group of followers in the formation of the Primitive Holiness Mission.

The association idea did not die with the further formation of sects, however, but it was forced to take a different focus. Since many participants were no longer members of the parent churches, they were not free to promote holiness inside those walls; so more attention was given to the development of the new denominations and less attention to the associations. Many of the local and regional organizations dropped out of existence entirely, and the National Holiness Association itself went through some very lean years and was forced to redesign its structure to include the new denominations. Recent developments reflect new vigor, and the change in name to Christian Holiness Association has opened the way to broaden both purpose and function. By 1983 fifteen religious bodies were currently members of the CHA with five other groups listed as "cooperating."[44]

The strength of the cooperative impulse among holiness people is reflected in the fact that hardly was the fragmenting process under way until the merging process began. The earliest development along this line was the bringing together of two holiness Mennonite groups in 1875 to form the United Mennonite church. In 1879 the addition of the Evangelical Mennonites made this the Evangelical United Mennonite church and in 1883 they united with the Brethren in Christ and took the name Mennonite Brethren in Christ. In 1947 this group became known as the United Missionary church and in 1969 joined with the Missionary Church Association to form the present Missionary church.[45]

The next major unifying effort came in 1895 when five separate holiness groups came together to form the Church of the Nazarene.[46] What later was to become the Pilgrim Holiness church developed as a result of no less that six separate mergers between 1919 and 1946.[47] In 1968 this group in turn merged with the Wesleyan Methodists to form the Wesleyan church. Other holiness groups produced by mergers are the Churches of Christ in Christian Union and the Evangelical Methodist church.[48] The most significant merger potential currently pending is between the Wesleyan church and the Free Methodists—a possibility that first came under discussion as early as 1903 when the Wesleyan Methodists and the Free Methodists first entered a long period of conversations and negotiations. At this writing, further developments along this line are not generally anticipated.

Beyond formal involvement at the top denominational level, many avenues of cooperative work among holiness groups have developed at the programmatic level. This has been particularly evident in the areas of publication, missions, and education. Through such agencies as the Holiness Denominational Publications Association, the Evangelical Foreign Missions Association (related to the National Association of Evangelicals), and such jointly sponsored educational institutions as Central Pilgrim College in Bartlesville, Oklahoma and Azusa Pacific University in Azusa, California, a wide spectrum of holiness bodies are finding ways to do things together in many cooperative ministries.

This review of the unity-division picture in the American holiness movement reveals an almost surrealistic pattern, which is complex and without design. It is a story of idealism and disillusionment, of schism and merger, of cooperation and competition, of independency and mutuality, of conflict and realignment, of tension and brotherly love.

Despite the incongruities, however, at least three prevailing themes emerge that give perspective to the thinking and action of the holiness leaders.

The first of these is that most of the promoters of holiness had no intention of making the doctrine a divisive issue. The often-stated and generally practiced policy was to witness *within* their own churches and to avoid even any suggestion toward schism. Their zeal for holiness, however, along with a degree of elitism, generated countervailing forces that resulted in opposition and sometimes ultimatums. That which they desired not to happen often came to pass, and division was the result—division that was rationalized as no fault of their own.

The second prevailing theme is that the doctrine of holiness is considered to be of greater importance that any denomination. This meant that holiness must not be contained within a single denomination: it also meant that denominational loyalties and commitments must be secondary to holiness teaching. The result was a de-emphasis on the church as institution and a consequent neglect of emphasis on the doctrine of the Church—including the unity of the Church. Consequently, even though Christian unity was valued by the leaders in the mainline holiness movement, it had a lower priority than correct teaching regarding sanctification and the holy life. Division that preserved this teaching was considered justifiable.

The third evident theme is the presence within the holiness movement of a significant number of leaders who linked holiness and unity together, making one the prerequisite of the other. Taking a strong stand against all division in the Church, branding it as sin to be purged by the Sanctifier, they challenged the whole Protestant pattern. They were branded as "come-outers" and accused of destroying the churches. They did preach, "Come out of her, my people," but they insisted they were not creating a new sect to divide the Church, further; they were simply inviting all the "saints" to enter into a great fellowship in the "church of God." This unity could be achieved as all the faithful left their dividedness behind. As a result of their deep aversion to the "sinful" sectarian system, all those holiness groups that hold to the "church of God" concept lost direct contact with the mainline holiness movement that gave either explicit or implicit sanction to denominationalism. Not only the Church of God (Anderson, Indiana) but also the Church of God (Holiness) and pentecostal groups such as the Church of God (Cleveland, Tennessee) and the Church of God in Christ have had only marginal relationships with the groups affiliated with the Christian Holiness Association.

This time in Christian history would seem to be especially propitious for all proponents of holiness to give major attention to the relational implications of the doctrine they value so highly, to the end that, under the leadership of the Holy Spirit, they may be able to give new impetus toward the unification of the whole church so that, indeed, the world may believe.

Notes

1. W. McDonald and John E. Searles, *The Life of Rev. John S. Inskip* (Chicago: The Christian Witness Co., 1885), 190.

2. G. Hughes, "The Vineland Encampment," *Guide to Holiness*, (September, 1867), 93.

3. As cited by Charles Edwin Jones, *Perfectionist Persuasion* (Scarecrow Press, 1974), 21.

4. This wording is from Article IV of the 1907 Constitution of the National Holiness Association. It is notable that by this date the "church question" was such that a parenthesis was added: "(unless reasonable circumstances forbid.)."

5. M. L. Haney, "Current Errors Among Teachers of Holiness," *Proceedings of the Western Union Holiness Convention*, p. 44.

6. C. J. Fowler, "President's Report . . ." *The Christian Witness* (June 11, 1908), p. 8, as quoted by Delbert R. Rose, *A Theology of Christian Experience* (Minneapolis: Bethany Fellowship, 1965), 75.

7. D. S. Warner, *Bible Proofs of a Second Work of Grace* (Goshen, Ind.: E. U. Mennonite Publishing Society, 1880), p. 397. It is notable that in the following year Warner disassociated himself from the organized holiness movement over the issue of its endorsement of sectarianism.

8. Delbert R. Rose refers to a 1952 interview with C. W. Butler, a long-time leader in the NHA, which reaffirms this strong transdenominational stance. (*A Theology of Christian Experience*, p. 76.).

9. Jesse T. Peck, *The Central Idea of Christianity* (Boston: Henry V. Degen, 1858), 326.

10. This view is well supported by Melvin E. Dieter, *Revivalism and Holiness* (Ann Arbor: University Microfilms, 1973), 231ff and by Jones, *Perfectionist Persuasion*, p. 54.

11. *Proceedings*, p. 21.

12. *Proceedings*, p. 23.

13. B. A. Washburn, "To the General Assembly, Chicago, May 20, 1885," *The Good Way*, VIII (May 23, 1885) quoted in Clarence Eugene Cowan, *A History of the Church of God (Holiness)* (Overland Park, Kan.: Herald and Banner Press, 1949), 24-25.

14. As quoted by John L. Peters, *Christian Perfection and American Methodism* (New York: Abingdon, 1956), 141.

15. William M. Greathouse, *Nazarene Theology in Perspective* (Kansas City: Nazarene Publishing House, 1970), 5.

16. Timothy L. Smith, *Called unto Holiness* (Kansas City: Nazarene Publishing House, 1962), 27.

17. Vinson Synan, *The Holiness-Pentecostal Movement in the United States* (Grand Rapids; Wm. B. Eerdmans, 1971), p. 37. He later observes (p. 53): "A measure of the intensity of the

Unity and Division

conflict over sanctification is the fact that twenty-three holiness denominations began in the relatively short period of seven years between 1893 and 1900." The process of schism did not end with the nineteeth century, however. Donald W. Dayton, in *The American Holiness Movement, A Bibliographical Introduction* (Wilmore, Ky: B. L. Fisher Library, 1971), p. 52, notes that very recent times have seen the formation of a number of new small holiness denominations. Included in these would be the Allegheny Methodist connection, the Bible Missionary church (originally Nazarene), the Wesleyan Holiness Association (originally Bible Missionary church), the United Holiness church, and the Evangelical Wesleyan church (both originally Free Methodist).

18. S. B. Shaw, ed., *Echoes of the General Holiness Assembly* (Chicago: S. B. Shaw, 1901), 275.

19. Shaw, p. 34.

20. As quoted and paraphrased by Delbert R. Rose, *A Theology of Christian Experience,* pp. 196-97.

21. Rose, p. 245.

22. John L. Peters, *Christian Perfection and American Methodism*, pp. 141-42

23. Timothy L. Smith (*Called unto Holiness,* p. 29) refers to *The Divine Church* by John P. Brooks as the textbook for "come-outism."

24. Data secured from Constant H. Jacquet, ed., *Yearbook of American and Canadian Churches, 1977* (Nashville: Abingdon, 1977), 8, 14.

25. S. B. Shaw, *Echoes*, p. 3

26. L. L. Pickett, *A Plea for the Present Holiness Movement* (Louisville: Pickett Publishing Co., 1896), p. 89.

27. Peck, *The Central Idea of Christianity*, p. 326.

28. John Wilkins, "Peace in Methodism," *Guide to Holiness*, 52 (November 1867), 144-45.

29. Adam Wallace, ed., *A Modern Pentecost: Embracing a Record of the Sixteenth National Campmeeting for the Promotion of Holiness Held at Landisville, PA, July 23 to August 1st, 1873* (Philadelphia: Methodist Home Journal Publishing House, 1873), 144. As quoted in Dieter, *Revivalism and Holiness*, p. 268.

30. *Proceedings*, p. 23.

31. As quoted by A. L. Byers, *Birth of a Reformation, or the Life and Labors of Daniel S. Warner* (Anderson, Ind.: Gospel Trumpet Co., 1921), 159.

32. D. S. Warner, *Bible Proofs of the Second Work of Grace* (Goshen, Ind.: E. U. Mennonite Publishing Society, 1880), 418-19.

33. Warner, pp. 421-22.

34. Warner, p. 425.

35. Warner, p. 427.

36. Warner, p. 427.

37. Warner, p. 428.

38. Warner, pp. 428-29.

39. Warner, p. 429.

40. Warner, pp. 431-32.

41. Warner, p. 436.

42. Donald W. Dayton, *The American Holiness Movement: A Bibliographical Introduction* (Wilmore, Ky.: B. L. Fisher Library, 1971), 52.

43. S. B. Shaw, *Echoes*, p. 9.

44. The 1983 member churches of CHA are these: Bible Holiness Movement, Brethren in Christ Church, Churches of Christ in Christian Union, Evangelical Church of North America, Evangelical Friends Alliance, Evangelical Methodist church, Free Methodist Church of North America, the Canadian Holiness Federation, the Church of the Nazarene, The Salvation Army, the Salvation Army in Canada, United Brethren in Christ Church, the Wesleyan church, Japan Immanuel Church. The cooperating

groups are the Church of God (Anderson, Indiana), the Missionary church, Methodist Protestant church, Primitive Methodist church, the Congregational Methodist church.

45. Further details of these developments may be found in Howard Albert Snyder, "Unity and the Holiness Churches," Unpublished B. D. Thesis, Asbury Theological Seminary, 1966, pp. 70-71.

46. For details see Timothy L. Smith, *Called to Holiness*.

47. Snyder, "Unity and the Holiness Churches," p. 70.

48. Snyder, p. 69.

John W. V. Smith

Context and Meaning
George Kufeldt

More than four hundred years ago, the reformer John Calvin wrote, "There are many statements in Scripture the meaning of which depends upon their context."[1] A child of the Renaissance, Calvin had been thoroughly schooled as a classical scholar. With his conversion, he continued to work within this humanist approach, and according to Rogers and McKim "adopted this contextual approach in the exegesis of Scripture. . . . He knew that this colored the text's meaning."[2]

Responsible interpreters of the Bible continue to follow the example and practice of Calvin, basing their exegesis of the biblical text upon the premise that "the first and weightiest rule of speech is that the context determines meaning."[3] To say it another way, "An exegesis which . . . disregards the context is quite inadequate."[4] The ability to handle the original languages and philology, the knowledge of the history, geography, and culture of the ancient world will count for little if the context of a Scripture passage is ignored. Indeed, to ignore the context almost inevitably leads to the misunderstanding, misinterpretation, and misuse of the Bible.

What is a context? The specific answers to this question vary according to the scholars' immediate aim or purpose. For example, William D. Thompson says, "A context consists of all the forces in motion around and upon the text. To put it that way is to eliminate the notion of text as a static entity and to see it as dynamic, moving, pulsating with life."[5] Thus, a context will not allow the text to be lifeless and meaningless. This happens, however, only so long as the context is allowed to function as it should. If the context is ignored, or is considered to be dead or meaningless, the text may either lose its meaning altogether, or worse, be given a meaning that is not intended at all by the writer or speaker.

One thing that can happen when the context is ignored is for the interpreter to take what Ralph P. Martin calls "the dogmatic approach,"[6] often referred to as "proof-texting." In this approach, says Martin, "the meaning of Scripture is atomized by being regarded as contained in key-words or key-phrases or isolated single verses treated without respect to their neighbouring context."[7] Such fragmentation cannot but destroy the intended meaning of a text, and so it results in the text becoming controlled by the subjective whims and ideas of the interpreter. This most serious charge is then made against this approach by Martin:

> And it is forgetful of God's providence in conveying his word to men not in fragmented or situation-less dicta, but in the total context of the historical milieu of an ancient people (Israel, the early church) and through the medium of a set of languages which make use of non-prescriptive modes of expression.[8]

A second pitfall into which the interpreter may fall if he or she ignores the context is "the impressionistic approach."[9] This error may be even more subtle since it may have the aura of "a more spiritual" attitude toward biblical revelation. Its main feature is that "the reader equates the message of the passages before him with the thoughts that fill his mind as he reads."[10] This treatment of Scripture easily leads

Context and Meaning

to cultism, growing out of the often rather bizarre interpretations that stem from human feelings and responses to texts because they now have lost their moorings in the objective realities of the context. A passage can easily have any one of several meanings if it is isolated from the living situation and time that it reflects. This approach also ignores the painful fact that the Bible is not always easily understood apart from serious effort and study. One must agree with Martin that the grammatico-historical method provides the much-needed antidote to these approaches. He says,

> The rigorous application of the grammatico-historical method will place a check on any tendency either to personal idiosyncrasy in wanting to read into the text what we wish it would say or a spiritualizing of the Bible which allows its message to float in an undefined vacuum and untethered to the historical events of the process of God's activity in salvation.[11]

In his answer to the question "What is a context?" George B. Caird notes that "the words we use have at least four types of setting, verbal, situational, traditional and cultural, all of which have an influence on their sense."[12] Since he describes the verbal context as "the sentence in which a word is used, the paragraph, the chapter or even the book,"[13] it may be better to limit the types of setting to three, for the verbal really becomes the vehicle of the situational, traditional, and cultural contexts, at least in the literary sense. Caird's own description of these three contexts also serves to support the preceding contention that the verbal context is not really separate but involves all three:

> The situational context includes such factors as the occasion of the utterance and the occupation of the speaker. If we wish to understand the sentence "There is something wrong with the table, we need to know whether the speaker is a housewife in the dining-room, a mason on a building site, a statistician in a computing laboratory or an official of the Water Board. The words "catholic", "orthodox" and "priest"

89

George Kufeldt

may be used by two speakers in very much the same situation, yet with a difference of sense because the speakers stand
in different traditions. The context of culture is important,
for example, to a Frenchman attempting to translate into his
own language the sentence, "I'm mad about my flat"; he
needs to know whether the speaker is an Englishman enthusiastic about his living-quarters or an American furious
about his puncture.[14]

Still another description of the nature of a context is
proposed and discussed by William D. Thompson.[15] The
five areas of context that he notes are these: historical,
political, proximate, theological, and cultural. He suggests
that "every biblical text has an historical context; that is,
something happened before and after it did."[16] While this
general principle is true and must be considered in interpreting any text, one must also be aware of the fact that often
texts such as wisdom and poetic passages do not have an
identifiable historical setting, thus limiting the usefulness of
this aspect of context. Also, one must be careful not to
stretch the limits or boundaries of a text's historical context
further than is really legitimate. Thompson is correct, especially as it relates to the biblical text, when he says that the
political context refers "not to any political party or point of
view but to the distribution of power in a society."[17] Because
it is true that "most of the Bible is written from the perspective of the powerless,"[18] the Bible is clearly "a word from the
Lord" to most of the world's people in every generation and
age.

The proximate context has to do with the immediate
textual context—what is being said immediately before and
after the passage one is interpreting. In a real sense, the
proximate context cannot be separated from any of the
other four context. It is not unlike Caird's verbal context,
referred to previously.

The theological context is especially relevant to the Bible
since it is first and last a theological book. So, one may say
that every text has some type of theological context, whether

Context and Meaning

proximate or more general. Often the theological context may really be a kind of general atmosphere that gave rise to or was the reason for the writing of a particular passage. As Thompson notes, for example, "the theological context of the creation account in Genesis is a world in which monotheism and polytheism were in serious combat."[19] It is the awareness of the theological context of the Genesis creation story that helps us appreciate its purpose and importance, and it also saves us from falling into the trap of trying to fit the biblical creation account into a rigid scientific framework. The theological context stresses the *who* and not the *how* of creation.

The cultural context provides the needed insight into the life and times, customs, and art, as well as the daily routines of the people from whom and by whom the biblical text has come to us. In order to understand what the Bible means to us today we must know something about what it meant to its original hearers/readers within the framework of their daily life and religious experience. The importance of understanding the cultural background of the Bible's story and message is rightly stressed by Walter C. Kaiser, Jr., when he wrote, "Special emphasis must be placed on the *context* every time the exegete meets what is suspected of being a strictly cultural item."[20] All cultural items must be recognized as being means to understanding and not necessarily ends in themselves. The content and the form of the cultural items must be clearly identified, and then utilized only as appropriate and valid. For example, one may recognize that the Decalogue in Exodus 20 follows the basic form and pattern of the Hittite treaty-covenants. The content of Exodus 20, however, is completely different since it is concerned with relationships between Israel and Israel's God Yahweh, and relationships within Israelite society under their God. Yet, without the discovery of the Hittite treaty-covenants and their meaning in that cultural context, we would not really understand many of the details of Israel's covenant ties with God.

The importance of each and all of these five aspects of the context is surely beyond dispute by any serious interpreter of the Bible. To ignore any of them or to deal inadequately with them, as Thompson warns, "may keep the preacher from understanding the point of the text at all, or produce an interpretation which bears no resemblance to its probable meaning."[21] When this happens, those who expect to hear from God through this preacher will be grossly shortchanged and cheated. The waiting congregation, to say nothing of the Word of God, deserves much better treatment than that.

Having explored some of the basic principles concerning the meaning and use of the context in interpreting the Bible, some examples or illustrations of how the biblical context sheds needed light on particular words or passages would seem appropriate. The examples that are discussed in the following will in no sense exhaust the possibilities, but I hope they will reinforce the great importance of context for biblical interpretation.

One of the most important terms for the understanding of the Old Testament is the Hebrew verbal root *yāda'*, which occurs more than one thousand times in the text. It is typically translated by some aspect of the idea "to know," not so much to express intellectual apprehension as experiential or intimate knowledge.[22] Thus it is said in Genesis 4:1 that "Adam *knew* Eve and she conceived and bore Cain" (RSV). There are, however, as James Barr notes, "a number of places where this does not appear to give satisfactory sense,"[23] In these instances the context seems to require a different meaning, a meaning that can be supported by reference to the cognate languages still within the Semitic family as is Hebrew. While Barr notes at least five different cognates that have been suggested by various scholars in different passages (some of which I myself question),[24] reference will be made here to only one of the suggested cognates and the light it sheds on particular passages.

Almost fifty years ago, the British scholar D. Winton

Context and Meaning

Thomas began calling attention to this problem,[25] noting appropriate cognates. He suggested the Arabic cognate *wadi'a,* "To care for/about," as being the appropriate equivalent for certain contexts in which Hebrew *yāda'* is found. For example, a typical translation of Exodus 2:25 reads, "And God saw the people of Israel, and God knew their condition" (RSV). The problem is that the Hebrew text does not have the words "their condition," these additional words being supplied by the RSV translators because the verb "to know" requires some kind of object. Most other translators also felt that something had to be added to complete the sense, such as, "them" (KJV, Moffatt, NIV)[26] and "it" (*An American Translation,* NEB).[27] The Living Bible certainly lives up to its name as a paraphrase here: "He knew that the time had come for their rescue"![28] One interesting exception is the Jerusalem Bible, which ends the verse with, "and he knew," but adds the footnote, "The verse does not yield satisfactory sense; probably the end is missing."[29] However, all these conjectural additions are unnecessary and the problem of ending is effectively resolved when the meaning suggested by the Arabic cognate *wadi'a* is recognized. The Hebrew of Exodus 2:25 then makes beautiful sense: "God saw the people of Israel and *he cared*"!

Another context in which *yāda'* has been translated traditionally by "to know" is Psalm 1:6: "For the Lord knows the way of the righteous, but the way of the wicked will perish" (RSV). It seems more than a little redundant to speak of God's knowing the way of anyone, for as God, he knows all. More importantly, the verb "to know is hardly an appropriate parallel word for "to perish" when one considers the rules of Hebrew poetic parallelism[30] But, when the meaning suggested by the cognate *wadi'a* is supplied, it not only makes good sense in the context, but it furnishes an appropriate poetic antithetic parallelism: "The Lord *cares for* the way of the righteous, but the way of the wicked will perish"![31] Other contexts in which *yāda'* may be better translated by "to care for/about" rather than "to know" include

93

Psalm 9:10, 31:7, 37:18; Job 9:21; Proverbs 12:10, 29:7; and Hosea 7:9, as well as many others. In his discussion of Thomas's long time work involving *yāda'* and its possible meanings, Peter R. Ackroyd notes that "even now, the new understanding has not penetrated as far as one might have expected."[32] One cannot but agree and wonder with him why there has been so little impact upon even the most recent translations.

Another aspect of the importance of the context in understanding and interpretation involves those words that may sound exactly alike, but that have completely different meanings. Usually this problem arose when a text was dictated to a group of scribes and a scribe would have to choose between two words that sound alike but have different meanings. For example, if one heard the words "He pared pears," one might think "He paired pears." Generally, the context would clarify which meaning was intended, although with some homophones—words that sound alike—it is possible that either of them could make some sense in a particular context. Usually, however, only one meaning would make the best sense.

The Hebrew Bible provides a classic example of homophones in the Hebrew words that are both pronounced "lo," although in their written forms they are very different. Misunderstanding them involves the hearing only. When hearing the sound "lo" a scribe could hear *lō'* meaning "no/not," or he might hear *lô* meaning "to/belonging to him/it." Two examples of this homophone will be cited here, one in Isaiah 9:3 (Hebrew text 9:2) and the other in Psalm 100:3. These are especially noteworthy because as early as the period of the Masoretes (scribes who lived between the fifth and tenth centuries A. D. and who standardized the Old Testament Hebrew text) these two passages were questioned. The text has the word for "no/not," so the Masoretes, recognizing a problem, indicated in their footnote that it was to be read as "to/belonging to him/it," rather

Context and Meaning

than change the text. When one reads the various English versions, however, one could become quite confused because the various versions contradict one another. For example, the KJV reading of Isaiah 9:3 is "Thou hast multiplied the nation, and *not* increased the joy: they joy before thee according to the joy in harvest, and as men rejoice when they divide the spoil" (italics added for emphasis). Contrast, however, the RSV rendering of the first two lines of the verse: "Thou hast multiplied the nation, thou hast increased *its* joy" (italics added for emphasis). The emphasized words point up the problem already noted by the Masoretes, namely, that "not" clearly is inconsistent with the context that makes three positive references to joy. Thus, the Masoretes suggested "belonging to it" or "its" in their footnote, a suggestion now followed by the modern English versions, although it was ignored by the KJV and yet was in the Masoretic text long before.

The second example is very similar and is cited here to reinforce the importance of the context, as the Masoretes realized. The KJV translates Psalm 100:3, "Know ye that the Lord he is God: it is he that hath made us, and *not* we ourselves; we are his people, and the sheep of his pasture." The relevant second line, however, is translated by the RSV in accordance with the Masoretic footnote to read, "It is he that made us, and we *are his*." The emphasized words again reflect the Masoretic realization that *not* does not make the best sense here, and in the context of the total Old Testament concept of creation. God is always recognized without question as Creator of the human race, and never is any suggestion made in the Old Testament that human beings or anyone other than God was involved. So, as the Masoretes noted, because God made people, they *belong to him.* At least twice in the Hebrew Old Testament just the opposite happened; the word *lô*, "to him," was written by the scribe instead of *lō'*, "not," so the Masoretes called attention to it in a footnote. These mistakes in hearing are found in 1

Samuel 2:16 and 20:2. The context clearly calls for "not," and the KJV heeds the Masoretic footnote in 1 Samuel 20:2, as do the modern versions. In 1 Samuel 2:16, however, the KJV translators apparently assumed that the Hebrew text originally had both *lô*, "to him" and *lō'*, "no," and that *lō'*, "no," had been left out by the scribe by means of haplography, an error of the eye.[33] So the KJV translators restored the "missing" *lō'*, "no," putting their translation, "*Nay*," in italics as they always did with words that they added when they were not in their Hebrew text. In other words, when they translated the text as it had been transmitted to them, they discovered that it was inadequate for the context. They then chose to add rather than to follow the Masoretic suggestion in the footnote, which would have cleared up the problem. The Masoretic suggestion would appear to be a bit safer; at least by recognizing a homophony, the translator does not have to add another word to the text.

One of the important and thus frustrating aspects of any written text is that, apart from added stage directions, the reader usually has few clues to the voice inflections or "tonal gestures" that the writer intended. In the case of the Bible, much of which was originally given orally, one may reasonably believe that much of the real meaning and impact of its message came to the original hearers through the way the original messengers spoke the Word of God. One cannot but wonder at how much more meaningful the words of the prophets would be for us if we could actually hear how they inflected them! One may be certain that while the typical pulpit-reading of the Bible is done in a dull, monotonous voice and thus with little meaning today, it was not given this way to the original hearers.

Since we have only the written word, without its original living context, is there any means by which we can apprehend and understand the inflection and meaning of the original messenger of the Word of God?

It is my contention that even a written context, if its true

Context and Meaning

dynamics are recognized and understood, often can provide meanings that have otherwise been missed or misunderstood. Admittedly, this can open the door to some subjectivism, but this should be minimal if the interpreter is alert to this danger and gives serious attention to every aspect of the text's context.

The inadequacy of the written word to convey the feeling and sound of the spoken word is vividly and pointedly illustrated by the Apostle Paul as he wrote to the Galatians, "I wish I could be with you now; then I could modify my tone; as it is, I am at my wits' end about you" (Gal. 4:20, NEB). When the reader checks the total context of Paul's message to the church at Galatia, it is clear that Paul has written some very harsh words to them. In saying that he would like to speak to them face to face, Paul is not implying that he would change what he said, but rather, in Caird's words, "that it would all sound very different if they could hear the changing inflexions of his voice."[34]

There is no doubt that unless we keep the matter of voice inflection in mind, although the written record cannot convey it, the meaning context of the recorded saying of Jesus may be missed. Perhaps the clearest example of this is the response of Jesus to the Syrophoenician woman, "Let the children first be fed, for it is not right to take the children's bread and throw it to the dogs" (Mark 7:27, RSV). His words must have been said with at least a half-smile on his lips and a twinkle in his eyes and an obvious lilt to his voice, encouraging the woman to retort in kind, "Yes, Lord; yet even the dogs under the table eat the children's crumbs" (Mark 7:28, RSV)! To fail to see and understand this context for these words is to fail to see Jesus at his human best.

One of the most common consequences of taking verses out of context is that of misunderstanding them, to say nothing of misusing them. This has happened to Isaiah 1:18: "Come now, let us reason together, says the Lord: though your sins are like scarlet, they shall be as white as snow;

though they are red like crimson, they shall become like wool" (RSV). It is perfectly clear as one reads this verse, apart from any context, that this verse is a beautiful statement of the willingness of a gracious God to extend his forgiveness to any repentant sinner. Little wonder that it has become the theme of literally thousands of evangelistic sermons since the beginning of the Church! However, when one takes a serious look at the context of this verse, including the verses that preceded as well as the verses that follow it, one must conclude that this verse really cannot be compassionate in its tone. Indeed, verses 2 through 15 of this chapter are a blanket indictment of the people of Judah who have openly rebelled against God, grossly mistreated their brothers under the covenant, and then have had the audacity to come to the Temple with their hands red with the blood of their brothers, raising them in prayer as though God did not know or care! They have tried to substitute religious rites for right actions toward their brothers in need, but God has rejected their ritual as meaningless and contradictory. Verses 16 and 17 clearly set forth God's requirements for his acceptance of them; show your professed love for God by loving your brother; ritual acts must be confirmed by righteous deeds. Verse 18 then must have the ring of sarcasm or irony rather than sentimental compassion. In view of the context, God is saying, "Come on, now, let's think about it. Though your sins are like scarlet, shall they really be as white as snow? Though they are red like crimson, shall they really become like wool?" Verses 19 and 20 conclude, "[Only] if you are willing and obedient shall you eat the good of the land. But if you continue to refuse and rebel, you shall be devoured by the sword." One must ask if there are question marks in the Hebrew text here. The answer is no, nor does it have the grammatical indicator that Hebrew uses to indicate ordinary questions. Just as in English, however, Hebrew can take a positive statement and simply by the proper voice inflection turn it into a question. We have all done it and

Context and Meaning

heard it done many times. While we cannot hear Isaiah's voice ask the questions in this instance, it seems clear to me that the context requires and implies irony, expressing questions. As early as 1939 this verse was interpreted as expressing questions by A. R. Gordon, who translated the Book of Isaiah in the Smith-Goodspeed or American Translation of the Bible.[35]

Another case in which the expression of irony or even sarcasm seems to be demanded by the context is found in 1 Kings 22:15-16. The kings of Judah and Israel had just heard the four hundred false prophets predict victory for them in an impending battle against Ramoth-gilead, but it did not ring true. As a check, they sent for Micaiah. "And when he had come to the king, the king said to him, 'Micaiah, shall we go to Ramoth-gilead to battle, or shall we forbear?' And he answered him, 'Go up and triumph; the Lord will give it into the hand of the king. 'But the king said to him, 'How many times shall I adjure you that you speak to me nothing but the truth in the name of the Lord?' " (RSV). Moffatt clearly expresses the sarcasm required by the context when he translates: " 'Oh, march away and win', said Micaiah, 'for the Eternal will put it into the hands of the king!' " Again, one must hear what is said and how it is said beyond the straightforward prose narrative, and thus hear in context.

The final example illustrating the importance of context also involves a reexamination of the Hebrew text and its traditional translation. The passage is the familiar text of Micah 6:8, "He has showed you, O man, what is good; and what does the Lord require of you but to do justice, and to love kindness, and to walk humbly with your God?" (RSV). The context obviously consists of the first seven verses of this chapter, set forth in the form of a legal indictment (Hebrew *rîb*) that God has against Judah. God gives the nation an opportunity to respond to the indictment (v. 3), and to recall God's gracious acts toward it in the past as he

99

delivered its people from bondage and led them through the wilderness to the Promised Land. Verses 6 and 7 appear to be Judah's vocal response to God, appropriately indicated by quotation marks as direct speech in the RSV. Judah's response is in the form of a number of questions that seem to be searching for the correct response to God's grace: should Judah bring uncounted numbers of burnt offerings, literally rivers of oil sacrifices, or even its first-born sons? Verse 8 is usually interpreted as saying that God has already laid out the proper response, and that is right actions rather than rituals that may be many but meaningless.

A reexamination of the Hebrew text, however, suggests a slightly different translation of the opening phrase of verse 8, which may relate it to the context with a bit more meaning. The literal translation of the opening phrase is simple enough: "He-has-showed to-you man what-is-good." As indicated by means of hyphens, there are four thought units in the Hebrew, and it is readily seen that they can be easily interpreted in the usual or traditional manner: "He has showed you, O man, what is good" Two points must be made. First, the verb form in Hebrew as in some other languages, not only expresses action but includes the subject as well. The verb form indicates person, number, and gender. While the verb here indicates "he-has-showed," a slightly different form is used to express "she-has-showed," and so on. Second, the word *man* usually has been interpreted to be a term of address, a vocative form of the noun, and so has been translated "O man." However, Hebrew has no case system of nouns and thus no special vocative form of nouns. This makes it necessary to rely on the context in determining whether one should translate "man" or "O man." So, taking the Hebrew text exactly as it stands, "man" may be taken as the subject of the verb, resulting in a translation that to me gives even more meaning when seen against the context, especially verses 6 and 7: "Man has showed you what is good, but what does the Lord require of you?" Man, other people, may give all kinds of suggestions about how we ought to respond to God, as seen in verses 6 and 7, but the true answer to the question can come only from God. Only God can give us the final judgment about what we must do.

This essay has been offered as an expression of my growing conviction that the context must be seen as the first tool of biblical understanding and interpretation or it is inevitable that the Word of God will be wrongly divided, leading to disaster. More than that, as A. Berkeley Mickelsen has written, "Faithful adherence to context will create in the interpreter a genuine appreciation for the authority of Scripture."[36]

Notes

1. John Calvin, *Institutes of the Christian Religion*, IV, xvi:23, quoted in Jack B. Rogers and Donald B. McKim, *The Authority and Interpretation of the Bible: An Historical Approach* (New York: Harper and Row, 1979), 97. Another translation of this line reads, "There are many passages of Scripture whose meaning depends on their peculiar position." John Calvin, *Institutes of the Christian Religion*, Henry Beveridge, trans. vol. 2 (Grand Rapids: Wm. B. Eerdmans Publishing Co., 1972), 545.

2. Rogers and McKim, *Authority and Interpretation,* p. 97. For a good brief discussion of Calvin as a biblical interpreter, see pp. 89-127.

3. George B. Caird, *The Language and Imagery of the Bible* (Philadelphia: Westminster Press, 1980), 49.

4. R. T. France, "Exegesis in Practice: Two Samples," in I. Howard Marshall, ed., *New Testament Interpretation: Essays on Principles and Methods* (Grand Rapids: Wm. B. Eerdmans Publishing Co., 1977), 266.

5. William D. Thompson, *Preaching Biblically: Exegesis and Interpretation* (Nashville: Abingdon Press, 1981), 57.

6. Ralph P. Martin, "Approaches to New Testament Exegesis," in I. Howard Marshall, ed., *New Testament Interpretation*, 220.

7. Marshall, *New Testament Interpretation*, p. 220.

8. Marshall, pp. 220-21.

9. Marshall, p. 221.

10. Marshall, p. 221.

11. Marshall, p. 226. See pages 222-223 for a brief but pointed discussion of the grammatico-historical method.

12. Caird, *Language and Imagery*, pp. 49-50.

13. Caird, p. 50.

14. Caird, p. 50.

15. Thompson, *Preaching Biblically*, pp. 58-61.

16. Thompson, p. 58.

17. Thompson, p. 59.

18. Justo and Catherine Gonzalez, *Liberation Preaching* (Nashville: Abingdon Press, 1980), 35.

19. Thompson, *Preaching Biblically*, p. 60.

20. Walter C. Kaiser, Jr., *Toward an Exegetical Theology: Biblical Exegesis for Preaching and Teaching* (Grand Rapids: Baker Book House, 1981), 118.

21. Thompson, *Preaching Biblically*, p. 61.

22. See Francis Brown, S. R. Driver, and C. A. Briggs, *Hebrew and English Lexicon of the Old Testament* (Oxford: Oxford University Press, 1968), 393-95 for numerous examples.

23. James Barr, *Comparative Philology and the Text of the Old Testament* (London: Oxford University Press, 1968), 19.

24. Barr, pp. 19-23.

25. "The Root *yd'* in Hebrew," *Journal of Theological Stud-*

Context and Meaning

ies, XXXV:298-306; "The Root yd' in Hebrew, II," *Journal of Theological Studies*, XXXVI:409-421; "More Notes on the Root yd' in Hebrew," *Journal of Theological Studies*, XXXVIII:400-403.

26. James Moffatt, *The Moffatt Translation of the Bible* (London: Hodder and Stoughton, 1964); *The Holy Bible: New International Version* (Grand Rapids: Zondervan Bible Publishers, 1978).

27. J. M. P. Smith and Edgar J. Goodspeed, eds., *The Complete Bible: An American Translation* (Chicago: University of Chicago Press, 1939); *The New English Bible* (London; Oxford University Press, 1970).

28. *The Living Bible: A Paraphrase* (Wheaton, Ill.: Tyndale House, 1971).

29. *The Jerusalem Bible* (Garden City, N. Y.: Doubleday and Co. Inc., 1966).

30. For a good discussion of the principles and rules of Hebrew poetry, including parallelism, see N. K. Gottwald, "Hebrew Poetry," *Interpreter's Dictionary of the Bible*, vol. 3 (Nashville: Abingdon Press, 1962), 829-838.

31. The Revised Psalter now translates, "preserveth," an obvious extension of "to care for." See *The Revised Psalter*, D. Winton Thomas, gen. ed. (London: SPCK, 1964), p. 1. M. Dahood translates "shall safekeep," *Psalms I. Anchor Bible*, vol. 16 (Garden City: Doubleday and Co., 1960), 1.

32. Peter R. Ackroyd, "Meaning and Exegesis," *Words and Meaning: Essays Presented to D. Winton Thomas*, Peter R. Ackroyd and Barnabas Lindars, eds. (Cambridge: Cambridge University Press, 1968), 12.

33. "This is an omission which is made when the same letter occurs twice together, or two similar letters, groups of letters or words follow each other directly." Ernst Würthwein, *The Text of the Old Testament: An Introduction to the Kittel-Kahle Biblia Hebraica*, Peter R. Ackroyd, trans. (Oxford: Basil Blackwell, 1957), 72.

34. Caird, *Language and Imagery*, p. 54.

35. Smith and Goodspeed, *The Complete Bible: An American Translation.*

36. A. Berkeley Mickelsen, *Interpreting the Bible* (Grand Rapids: Wm. B. Eerdmans Co., 1963), 113.

The Nature of God
as the Basis for
Understanding Forgiveness
Fredrick H. Shively

FORGIVENESS IN THE SYNOPTIC GOSPELS

When Jesus, as Luke 23:34 records, looked from the cross upon the very people who put him there and asked the Father to forgive them, he stated in one brief prayer the essence of the Christian gospel. Jesus' statement is a culmination of a life devoted to teaching and exemplifying the meaning of forgiveness.

F. F. Bruce says, "The story of Jesus is the message of salvation."[1] While holding the infant Jesus, Simeon proclaimed that his eyes had seen salvation, prepared in the sight of and for all people (Luke 2:30-32). Luke carries this theme of universal salvation further than do the other evangelists. When he records the Isaiah 40:3-5 prophecy in reference to John the Baptist, he includes more of the quotation than do the others, adding that "all mankind will see God's salvation" (Luke 3:6; cf. Isa. 40:5).

Jesus inaugurates his ministry in the Nazareth synagogue

with the reading of Isaiah 61:1-2: "The Spirit of the Lord is on me, because he has anointed me to preach good news to the poor. He has sent me to proclaim freedom for the prisoners and recovery of sight for the blind, to release the oppressed, to proclaim the year of the Lord's favor" (Luke 4:18-19). This statement of purpose highlights the positive thrust of Jesus' ministry to and for people: good news, freedom, and sight. It concludes with the pronouncement of a spiritual jubilee year, obviously stopping just short of Isaiah's next words, "The day of vengeance of our God" (Isa. 61:21). When Jesus replied to John's inquiry as to whether or not he was the one they expected, he pointed to what had happened: "The blind receive sight, the lame walk, those who have leprosy are cured, the deaf hear, the dead are raised, and the good news is preached to the poor" (Luke 7:22). Could this be a fulfillment of Isaiah 53:4ff? If it is, once again Jesus stopped just short of including "God will come with vengeance."

Jesus' message is one of hope and deliverance. In Luke special consideration is given to the underprivileged—the poor, women, Samaritans, tax collectors, and sinners. This message of mercy and salvation underscores the permeating reality of the forgiveness of God in Christ. While *repentance* is the first word of the gospel, *forgiveness* is its culminating and all-consuming word.

The truth of James Emerson's statement "The heart of the good news is the fact of forgiveness—not as a doctrine but as an experience"[3] is that forgiveness should be given the central place in the ministry of the Church. It is necessary, however, that we establish this fact by a careful study of the scriptural record. Whether or not Emerson's statement is a fact, or whether or not one comes to know the experience, depends upon the work of the Spirit in a person's life. Helmut Thielicke says,

Truth may well be the same as that which discloses itself,

> which enlightens, and which is thus intelligible, and we can accept this in relation to God's truth. It, too, is disclosure, being evident. But the question is, for whom is it disclosed, and to whom is it evident?[4]

Thielicke asserts that this truth is concealed from the natural person. It is known only to God and to those to whom God reveals it, those who are open to receive and experience this truth.

The message of the Scriptures is that the Word of God and the Son of God meet in the person of Jesus Christ, that Jesus came to reveal the Father and his nature. His coming was dramatic, unexpected in its manner, and decisive. He both spoke and was the Word of God. He was God's representative, bearing the Father's seal of approval and exercising divine authority as God's Son.

His teachings, miracles, relationships and particularly his passion combine to express the Father's word and will to the world. Thielicke has written,

> Where do we meet the decisive, active Word? A provisional answer to this question is that we meet it when it strikes us as an effectual Word in the sense that in the law and the gospel it breaks off the old existence and starts a new one, bringing sins to light and forgiving them, changing God's rejection into an acceptance which gives me a new future and makes me a new creature in the miracle of the Spirit.[5]

It is a word, Thielicke says, "which we can know, which applies to us and which understands us before we can understand it."[6] As the Word enlightens and explains us, it becomes evident that we benefit enormously from it. This Word literally sets us free.

All true theology is rooted in the nature of God. We human beings are able to know or understand only those aspects of God's nature that he chooses to reveal to us. The open, revealing side of God meets persons and works in us, enabling us to be the creative, active, living, people who are able to relate to one another. Only by entering into such

107

relationships can we come to know God. At best, this knowledge is limited.

As we think of God, then, we are in need of images or analogies to relate to him. Jesus provided these images or analogies for us.

Jesus' purpose was to reveal God to us. So Jesus is the truest way to understand God, and thus to understand ourselves as well. Jesus came at a particular time in history to a particular culture. In order to understand the transcendent nature of God as it comes through the Incarnation, we must peer through each analogy to understand its perspective, and to allow it to reveal to us the greater truth about God that lies behind it.

Jesus did not attempt to prove God's existence. At all times he acted upon belief in it, entering into a lively relationship of trust, prayer, and obedient service. As Jews, Jesus' hearers also acted upon trust, having learned as children to recite the Shema, "Hear O Israel: The Lord our God, the Lord is One" (Deut. 6:4). The question that remained was, What is God like? At this point conflict arose, because the picture of God that Jesus painted was not the same as that within the minds of the people.

What was different? Jesus used traditional terms such as *king* and *judge* to describe God, but he reserved as primary the designation "Father."

For Jesus to call God Father had a special meaning. Although Jesus did not call himself "Son of God," he admitted sonship in his frequent references to his Father. To call God Father speaks of Jesus' mission in the world to represent the Father and to make him known. Joachim Jeremias has summarized Jesus' teachings:

> In attempting to recover the original significance of the parables, one thing above all becomes evident: it is that the parables of Jesus compel His hearers to come to a decision about His personal mission. For they are all full of "the secret of the Kingdom of God," (Mark 4:11), that is to say, the

recognition of "an eschatology that is in process of realization." The hour of fulfillment is come, that is the urgent note that sounds through them all. The strong man is disarmed, the forms of evil are in retreat, the physician comes to the sick, the lepers are cleansed, the great debt is wiped out, the lost sheep are brought home, the door of the Father's house stands open, the poor and the beggars are summoned to the banquet, a master whose kindness is undeserved pays his wages in full, a great joy fills all hearts. God's acceptable year has come. For he has been manifested whose veiled glory shines through every word and through every parable—the Savior.[7]

Jesus' greatest challenge was to break through the prejudice, fear, and ignorance of people so that they might understand his images of God. We can know God conceptually only by metaphor or analogy. To say that God is a loving Father is metaphorical. It helps us to understand the nature of God, but we cannot draw the use of this analogy too far; for example, to say that every father is like God is to limit God within fatherhood. Jesus also refers to the shepherd who lost a sheep and the woman who lost a coin in speaking of God (Luke 15:8-10). To say that God is either male or female is again to limit God. We are the ones who are limited by being forced to choose one over the other to refer to him, by the use of the masculine pronoun.

To speak of the "heart" of God is also metaphorical. The Scriptures suggest that God "speaks" or that with his "finger" he "writes." To say that God has a heart is to suggest that God "feels" or experiences emotion in relating to humankind. In using such terms we are attempting to understand God by virture of our own inner life. We cannot speak of God without metaphors, and yet God transcends all of our attempts to describe him.

That Jesus accomplished the task of breaking through the prejudice and ignorance of some is a tribute not only to his teaching, but also to his commitment to live out this teaching. He lived as a Son of the Father, always longing to please him. All three Synoptists record the Father's blessing on the Son, first at the baptism, the inauguration of Jesus' public ministry (Matthew 3:17), and then on the Mount of Transfiguration, the point in Jesus' ministry at which he turned toward the cross (Matt. 17:5; Mark 9:7; Luke 9:35).

Jesus' references to God as Father began with his first recorded boyhood statement (Luke 2:49) and concluded with Luke's final words for him, "Father into your hands I commit my spirit" (Luke 23:46). To think of God as Father was not completely unfamiliar to the people of Israel. The writer of Exodus told of God's words to Moses, "Then say to Pharoah, 'This is what the Lord says: Israel is my firstborn son' " (Exod. 4:22). And the psalmist wrote, "As a father has compassion on his children, so the Lord has compassion on those who fear him" (Ps. 103:13).

Jesus introduced some key differences, however. He was the first to address God as "my Father" and he taught his disciples to pray "our Father." James Stewart points to two respects in which this teaching was original. First, Jesus made it the center of all his teaching, and second, he gave to the term new depth and content.[8]

In the Old Testament God is the Father of Israel in the sense that he is the founder and creator of the nation.[9] God has created all people, but he has adopted Israel as a son (Hos. 11:1). Later Rabbinic teaching recognized God as father.[10] Although the New Testament's teaching is not new, there is an added dimension to its use of the term. Manson states,

> Moreover, one has only to read the New Testament to realize that "the Father" was not a mere article in a creed or just a title for God, but a burning conviction, a spiritual experience which gave new meaning and value to life, and brought new peace and joy to human hearts.[11]

Of all the titles for God, the supreme title is *Father*.[12] What are its meanings? First, the Father is concerned about his children. If earthly fathers can do good for their children, how much more does God care for his? (Matt. 7:11). This concern allows the children to trust the Father. Second, the Father knows and understands each person, so that "the very hairs of your head are all numbered" (Matt. 10:30). Third, the Father wants his children to come to him in prayer. We have direct access, the curtain of the Temple having been torn in two (Matt. 27:51). We are urged to ask, seek, and knock, and to persist in so doing (Matt. 7:11).

Fourth, God's Fatherhood brings a new light to sin and forgiveness. Jesus taught us to ask God for forgiveness (Matt. 6:12) and told us that if we expect God to forgive us, then we must be ready to forgive one another. Fifth, since God is our Father, we are sisters and brothers. We come together in him. When we call God Father, how can we not forgive our sisters and brothers? Stewart phrases it this way:

> If the power behind the universe were sheer impersonal law, then our wrong thoughts and deeds would be sins against law. But if the power behind the universe is as Jesus revealed, a Father, then our wrong thoughts and deeds are sins against love. To call God Father is ultimately to make sin intolerable.[13]

George Ladd points out in *A Theology of the New Testament* that, although the God of the prophets was active both in judging and saving and the God of late Judaism was no longer working redemptively, "in Jesus, God has taken the initiative to seek out the sinner, to bring lost men into the blessing of His reign, Heaven, in short, the seeking God."[14] Ladd further identifies God as seeking, inviting, fatherly, and judging.[15]

Jesus says in his summation of the encounter with Zacchaeus, "For the Son of Man came to seek and to save what was lost" (Luke 9:10). The human experience is one of lostness. God takes the initiative, seeking until he finds the lost one. The lost individual has great value. Again Ladd says it very well:

> At the very heart of our Lord's message and mission was embodied the reality of God as seeking love. God was no

111

longer waiting for the lost to forsake his sins; God was
seeking out the sinner.[16]

Luke 15 contains three stories from Jesus about lostness,
no doubt a deliberate grouping by the evangelist. Jesus was
attempting to answer his critics' complaints about his wel-
coming sinners to table fellowship. Divine initiative is in
each parable. The shepherd leaves his sheep to find the one
that is lost and rejoices after having found it. Luke concludes, "There is more rejoicing in heaven over one sinner
who repents than over ninety-nine righteous persons who do
not need to repent" (Luke 15:7). Likewise, the woman gives
all of her careful energy to find the one lost coin.

The last of the three stories is Jesus' longest parable and
presents the crowning picture of God in all of the Synoptics.
Ladd says, "The heart of the Kingdom of God was Jesus'
inner experience of God as Father."[17] Barclay terms this
story "the very essence of the faith."[18] Manson calls it "the
Parable of the Father's love" and says, "The parable describes with touching simplicity what God is like, His goodness, His grace, His boundless mercy, His abounding love."[19]
Thielicke's preferred title is "The Waiting Father."[20] The
parable tells of the son and his profligate living and how, all
the while, the Father waits and longs for his safe return.
When finally the father recognizes the familiar profile on the
horizon, he lays all dignity aside, runs to greet his returning
son, and calls for the greatest celebration possible. Steward
encapsules this moment of meeting:

> Daringly Jesus pictured God, not waiting for his shamed
> child to slink home, nor standing on his dignity when he
> came, but running out to gather him, shamed and ragged
> and muddied as he was, to his welcoming arms.[21]

The word *forgiveness* does not appear in any of the three
stories, but the meaning is inherent. God, as Father, has put
away condemnation and exhibited forgiveness.

Two other parables deserve attention, the two debtors

Understanding Forgiveness in the Gospels

(Luke 7:41-43) and the unmerciful servant (Matt. 18:21-36). Jesus told the first while he was being honored in the home of Simon the Pharisee. Perhaps he had just preached a sermon that had impressed them. A woman seen as a sinner spontaneously expressed her grateful love for the forgiveness Jesus had pronounced for her. To the shock and dismay of the party guests, Jesus received all of this attention gladly, and when challenged, told the story of the two debtors owing differing amounts. Having their debts canceled, which was more grateful? As a debtor herself, the woman owed more, was forgiven more, and was more grateful. She was nearer to God than were the party guests. In contrast, the unmerciful servant in the second parable displays his lack of gratitude and generosity. Having been forgiven a great sum, he is unwilling to forgive another a small debt. The master who forgave him is incensed and withdraws his own graciousness. The proper response to grace, then, is gratitude. When forgiven, a person is freed and enabled to forgive others. As Barclay says, "If we could enter into real fellowship with God we must learn by His grace to forgive as he forgives."[22]

Barclay goes on to tell of a Rabbinic saying that urges one to forgive three times but not the fourth.[23] Perhaps Peter, then, in asking how many times to forgive, thought that forgiving another seven times went far beyond the necessary. But Jesus' admonition is to forgive without end (Matt. 18:22). The generous spirit of forgiveness has come full circle from its direct opposite found in Genesis 4:24, "If Cain is avenged seven times, then Lamech seventy-seven times." Unlimited vengeance has become unlimited forgiveness.

Jesus' teaching expresses concern for the sinner. His mission is to minister to sinners. He takes sin and sinners seriously. Jesus' common expression for sinners is, as in the parables previously noted, the lost (Matt. 10:6; 15:24; 18:11). Some are lost like sheep, heedless; some, like the coin, by circumstance; some, like the son, deliberately. He loves them all.

This concern for the sinner is new sentiment in Judaism. One Jewish writer had stated,

> For indeed I will not concern myself about the fashioning of those who have sinned, or about their death, their judgment, or their destruction; but I will rejoice over the creation of the righteous, over their pilgrimage also, and their salvation.[24]

Jeremias states Jesus' nontraditional relationship to sinners beautifully:

> Again and again they ask: "Why do you associate with this riffraff, shunned by all respectable people." And He replies: "Because they are sick and need me, because they are truly repentant, and because they feel the gratitude of children forgiven by God. Because, on the other hand, you, with your loveless, disobedient hearts, have rejected the gospel. But, above all, because I know what God is like, so good to the poor, so glad when the lost are found, so overflowing with a father's love for the returning child, so merciful to the despairing, the helpless, and the needy. That is why!"[25]

Sin is a serious matter to the Synoptists. As Guthrie points out, it is universal, internal, enslaving, and rebellious, meriting of condemnation.[26] The term used most frequently in the New Testament, *hamartia*, means "missing the mark." It implies an awareness of what is expected and the realization that one has not achieved it. John the Baptist did not have to explain sin to his listeners; they knew its meaning. *Paraptoma*, "trespass"; *opheiloma*, "indebtedness"; and *anomia*, "lawlessness," a term used only by Matthew, are other common expressions. The last term implies hostility toward God. Jesus applied it to those who claim to be righteous (Matt. 7:22-23).

The word *sin* is found frequently in accounts of the healing of the paralytic (Matt. 9:1-8; Mark 2:1-12; Luke 5:17-26). Jesus dares to pronounce to this man forgiveness of sin, demonstrating the power of God, the priority of God, and the person-centeredness of God. God is able to forgive sins as well as to heal, and he places the greater value on freeing a person from his or her sins.

Jesus recognized the terrible effects of sins: separation from God the Father, enslavement, guilt. He sees sin to be the breaking of an inner law (Matt. 5:21, 27). Sin represents what a person is (Matt. 15:18ff). It breaks the heart of God (Matt. 23:27). Jesus did not minimize the seriousness of sin, although some thought he did. He was able, however, to separate the sin from the sinner. He understood the meaning of lostness. He was called the "friend of sinners" (Matt. 11:9).

Many questions have been raised in people's minds regarding the unpardonable sin (Mark 3:28ff; Matt. 12:31-32; Luke 12:10). Jesus' words are that whoever blasphemes against the Holy Spirit will not be forgiven. Jesus sees that some allow their hearts to harden so that their judgment is impaired. They lose the power to recognize goodness; they do not know that it is God who comes to them. Ladd says it this way:

> When a man has become so blind that he cannot distinguish between the power of God's kingdom and the working of the devil but thinks that the kingdom of God is demonic, that person can never be forgiven.[27]

Simply put, the unpardonable sin is a refusal to accept God's forgiveness.

God's forgiveness is free, but the person must receive it in order to experience its effects. Contrary to many twentieth-century psychologists who suggest that the answer to sin is an assertion of the self and a denial of guilt, Jesus proclaims only one answer for sin, repentance. Repentance is a turning to God. The sinner acknowledges spiritual bankruptcy, trusts God for the gift of forgiveness, and responds with joy and gratitude. Grace and truth go together (John 1:14). Thielicke says, "Whenever the New Testament speaks of repentance, always the great joy is in the background."[28] Jesus' call to repentance is an invitation to accept God's forgiveness and to experience joy.

In his teachings Jesus challenges his disciples to be mercy-givers, not judges. He says, "Do not judge, or you too will be judged" (Matt. 7:1). We simply are not able to know everything about a person. The Old French proverb says, "To know all is to forgive all." Those who are forgiven gratefully set out to forgive others.

One of the most important verses for our consideration of God's nature is Matthew 5:48, "Be perfect, therefore, as your heavenly Father is perfect." These words have perplexed many who had tried in vain to be perfect and, when they were honest, admitted that they had not achieved perfection. The verse states that we are to be like God. What, then, is the meaning of "perfect"? The key to understanding is in the Lucan parallel. In exactly the same context, relating to one's enemies, the injunction reads, "Be merciful, just as your Father is merciful" (Luke 6:36). To be *merciful* is to fulfill the perfection and, thus, to be like God. And it is the merciful, Jesus says, who receive mercy (Matt. 5:7).

Rall has delineated three stages in the Christian's understanding of God.[29] One, the lowest, is that he is power; two, that he is just; and three, that he is pure and perfect good will. Within the person, these stages become first, mere might, which is selfish; second, bald justice, loving those who love you and retaliating against evil; and third, becoming the child of God, forgiving as God forgives.

Jesus forgives from the cross because his dying is in itself the high cost of forgiveness. In his humiliation and death, he takes on himself the sins of the world. Jesus himself connects the forgiveness of sins with his death. As he said, "The Son of Man did not come to be served, but to serve and to give his life as a ransom for many" (Matt. 20:28). At the Last Supper, he told the disciples, "This is my blood of the covenant, which is poured out for many for the forgiveness of sins" (Matt. 26:28). Steward adds, "He knew that the same cross that uncovered the sin of man would also reveal the very heart of God."[30]

By his actions, Jesus calls us to follow his example. Manson depicts it thus:

> The moral ideal for Christians lies not in a code, nor in a social order. It is in a life when love to God and Man is the spring of every thought and word and action; and for Christians the sum of all morality is to have the same mind which was also in Jesus.[31]

FORGIVENESS IN THE GOSPEL OF JOHN

The Gospel of John is the gospel of Father and Son. It focuses on salvation by revelation. The Son has come to make the Father known. In order to understand the Father, we must understand the Son. John A. T. Robinson believes that no other New Testament document is more important for studying the Jewish sources of the "Son of God" than the Fourth Gospel.[32]

The purpose of John's gospel is clearly stated in the text, and it brings together Jesus' sonship with his messianism. "These are written that you may believe that Jesus is the Christ, the Son of God, and that by believing you may have life in his name" (John 20:31). The proximate goal is faith, and the ultimate goal is life. John "is sure that God has acted, and that his action is seen supremely in Jesus Christ," writes Leon Morris.[33]

The faith that John portrays is not vague; it is concrete, centering in the person of Jesus as both the fulfillment of the hope of the Jewish people and as the very representative of God. This is more of a Messiah than the Jews had looked for, so John's Gospel is a running polemic with the Jews. With John there is no question. In the words of Thomas, Jesus is "my Lord and my God" (John 20:28). Faith in Christ is the way to abundant life (John 10:10). It is the way to the Father (John 14:6).

Colwell and Titus write, "In the Johannine Gospel Jesus is

not one among several revelations of God; He is *the* Revelation."[34] In the prologue, John identifies the Word and God. In verse fourteen the evangelist says that the Word is the Son who came from the Father. John the Baptist is not the revelation. Judaism is not the revelation. John's Gospel is an invitation for us to "come and see" (John 1:30; 1:46; 4:29), to experience him for ourselves. John makes the very strong claim, "No one has ever seen God, but God the only Son, who is at the Father's side, has made him known" (John 1:18).

Though charged with being the revelation of God, Jesus does not claim equality with God (John 4:19ff). Rather, he asserts the Son's dependence upon the Father. He is the picture of an obedient Son. Jesus claims that the authority he has is not self-derived; it is the Father's authority. The Father loves the Son and gives authority to him. The relevation is God's. To miss the Son is to miss the Father and to fall into danger, because judgment has been given by the Father to the Son.

That which saves is hearing and believing in God, who sent Christ. The one who believes will not be condemned but will be given life. Life is John's constant theme. Jesus is the water of life (John 4:14); the bread of life (John 6:35); the way, the truth, and the life (John 14:6); the resurrection and the life (John 11:25). It is the Father's will that everyone enjoy this gift of life (John 6:40). Further, no one can come to the Son unless the Father draws him or her (John 4:44; 6:65). This divine enabling eliminates all pretense of self-salvation. Salvation is from God, and Jesus is the only way to receive it (John 14:6).

In his Gospel, the evangelist illustrates this truth with several pastoral dialogues in which Jesus engaged. Nicodemus, a member of the Sanhedrin, came to Jesus secretly, seeking to understand Jesus' message better (John 3:1-15). Jesus' reply was startling. He called for the necessity of new birth, a spiritual birth that allows a new beginning in life.

Understanding Forgiveness in the Gospels

The implications are magnificent for our understanding of forgiveness. This new beginning is granted because of God's love for all persons. It is "the world" that God loves, and the invitation is universal; "whoever believes" shall be saved (John 3:16). It is not God's purpose to condemn the world. If condemnation comes, it comes because a person refuses to receive the proffered gift of grace.

Jesus' dialogue with the woman at the well caused consternation among his disciples, but it meant a drink of the water of life for the Samaritan woman (John 4:1-42). Despite knowing her background and her sinfulness, he in no way rejected her but, rather, offered her a great gift. As she talked to Jesus, faith grew in her until it came to the point of commitment. Because of this woman's testimony, many others in the town came to believe for themselves.

After Jesus healed the invalid who had lain by the Pool of Bethesda, he urged him to stop sinning (John 5:14). A healed, redeemed life is to be lived in glory to God.

The account of the woman caught in the act of adultery is not found in the oldest manuscripts (John 7:53—8:11). Only D gives it much support.[35] But as Morris says, "If we cannot feel that this is part of John's Gospel, we can feel that the story is true to the character of Jesus."[36] It finds a resonant note of response within us. It accords so well with what else we know of Jesus and it speaks to our human condition. The woman brought to Jesus was caught in the act of adultery. Someone must have seen her, because the conditions for charging her with adultery were extremely stringent. Having brought the woman before the whole crowd, the Pharisees intended to embarrass Jesus.

The penalty for such an act was death, although the accusers were stretching the law to make it fit only the woman. But if Jesus said, "Stone her," he would be breaking Roman law. If he said, "Let her go," he would be breaking the law of God. It was a vicious trap. After writing in the sand, Jesus invited those without sin to throw the first stone.

119

He did not say that no stones should be thrown; he simply appealed to conscience and called for fairness. Who was then innocent enough to be her accuser? When no one remained to condemn her, Jesus said, "Neither do I condemn you. Go now and leave your life of sin" (John 8:11). He offered her not simply forgiveness, but also abundant mercy with both the injunction and the enabling to live a righteous life.

Jesus had many discourses with the Pharisees. In chapter 8, John records their insistence that they are Abraham's children (John 8:31-59). Jesus denies this, because they do not recognize him. How can they claim that God is their Father when they do not recognize Jesus, who came from the Father? In this account Jesus faces a two-fold evil: traditional mind-sets and sinful hearts, embodying the twin evils of prejudice and malice. He attacks them equally as enemies of truth and right; they are both binding and deceptive. The Jews are bound by an inadequate understanding of Abraham's true descendants in the faith. They are bound by their own defensiveness. seeing Jesus as a threat to their power and authority. To his disciples Jesus comments, "If you hold to my teaching, you are really my disciples. Then you will know the truth, and the truth will set you free" (John 8:32). The Pharisees were not free to see. They looked at the blind man and saw a sinner who deserved his condition (John 9:13-41). Jesus looked at the blind man and saw a person in need of healing.

Understanding the nature of God in John's Gospel, as with the Synoptics, does not depend only on what Jesus said, but upon what he did. He loved, healed, and forgave, but primarily, he died for the sins of the world. "The good shepherd," he said "lays down his life for the sheep" (John 10:11). Jesus went through the Passion to the cross and died willingly. His death was the fulfillment of his ministry. As his life revealed the Father's love—enormous love for the world.

Understanding Forgiveness in the Gospels

The Resurrection revived the disciples' faith, filled them with understanding, and launched them into mission, a mission of caring for the sheep with tenderness and compassion (John 21:15-19). Jesus breathed into them the gift of the Holy Spirit and commissioned them to a ministry of forgiveness (John 20:23).

One incident in John's account deserves a closer look. This story, unique to John's Gospel, gives us deep insights into the nature of God and into the appropriate response that we are called to make to the way God shows himself to us. When Jesus knew that the time for him to depart from this world was very near, he was concerned that his hand-picked disciples be prepared to take the message of salvation to all the world. Moreover, Jesus loved these men deeply and was eager for them to know the richness of the full life. More than once they had demonstrated to him their lack of understanding of his message and purpose. This same lack of understanding is often true of the Church today. How often Jesus' compassion must cause him to weep as he did at the tomb of Lazarus because we allow our shortsightedness to cloud our understanding!

Thus, John records that Jesus took the Twelve to the Upper Room to impress his teachings more firmly upon their hearts and prepare them for the tragic days soon to follow. Following the account of Jesus' washing of his disciples feet in John 13, the next four chapters record his intimate teaching to and supreme love for these who were chosen to witness of him to the world. In essence, Jesus was taking them into a new depth of relationship with their Lord.

During the meal, Jesus arose, poured water into a pail, tied a towel around his waist, and began to wash the disciples' feet. Why did he do this? What was he trying to teach? Was he initiating a sacramental service?

Some have speculated that this act is symbolic of the Lord's Supper because John does not include the supper itself as do the other evangelists. Others see a comparison to baptism, particularly in connection with the washing of Peter's feet. However, neither of these views finds much basis in this passage. It would seem that Jesus was not inaugurating any kind of sacrament as such, but, rather, he was attempting to teach a basic lesson in true greatness, which must include humility. Furthermore, he was trying to break down the barriers existing within them so that they might participate fully in the fellowship of love. Only in this spirit could Christ communicate to them his great concern and the urgency of their mission.

He must have been responding to an immediate need, because he arose before they had finished eating. Perhaps something wrong had to be made right. Perhaps not all was serene in the interrelationships of these men. We can suppose that as they walked together on the dusty roads, they had occasion to press their own claims, each to the other. Judas was not the only one who still had visions of a physical kingdom. We know from other occasions that they were concerned about precedence of rank. Ruffled feelings could easily ensue.

Perhaps, on other occasions as they ate together, it was customary to take turns washing one another's feet. We can assume, however, that on this occasion they had not done this menial task. We can picture them sitting around the table, feet tired and dirty, and the atmosphere sullen and clouded. This hampered Jesus' task. At this point, he left his meal to show them the true spirit of community.

No doubt the reactions of the Twelve were varied. Certainly, they were surprised and greatly dismayed. To see their beloved Master working his way on his knees from man to man simply, silently, and lovingly must have cut them to the heart. For in this act the greater humility is not the washing of the other's feet but having one's own feet washed and realizing in one's heart that he does not deserve such love.

Understanding Forgiveness in the Gospels

In the tense silence, we can see each man cringing, miserable, as Jesus approached him. Slowly, the love that he was showing permeated the room and their hearts; they were becoming a community again.

Let us take a closer look at two of these disciples, Judas and Peter. The Scripture does not tell us what Judas' reaction was, but we know that he already had it in his heart to betray the Master. As Jesus approached him, no doubt Judas thought of his recent arrangement with the authorities to lead them to Jesus at a good time so as not to raise a disturbance. They had told him that Jesus was a madman, and he thought so also. Did he entertain doubts as Jesus came nearer?

Jesus knew what was in Judas' heart. I think that he longed to win this man who could have been a great evangelist. It is very possible that we could have had a gospel according to Judas. As Jesus washed the feet of Judas, he knew that there was something far more important that having clean feet: having a clean heart. But as much as he loved Judas, he could not and would not rob him of his free will. And Judas remained unchanged. That is why Jesus said, "You are not all clean."

As Jesus came to Peter, he met a typical Petrine response. This action was more than Peter could stand. Never tongue-tied, he blurted out, "Lord, do *you* wash *my* feet?" In this question, and in Jesus' answer, "What I am doing *you* do not know now," we see a strong emphasis upon personal pronouns. Certainly Peter loved Jesus, but this was not his image of his relationship with his Lord. What Peter failed to see is that, rather than showing humility, he was demonstrating his lack of it. Furthermore, Jesus was teaching him that obedience is a necessary part of love, even when one does not understand.

As Jesus finished, surely the atmosphere had changed to an air of submission and warmth. The disciples' heads must have nodded in a growing understanding as he explained his actions to them. The mere fact that their fellowship grew and their love increased demonstrates their awareness of what Jesus was doing. Peter, in his first epistle, encourages the believers not to strike back under fire, but says simply, "Put on the apron of humility" (1 Pet. 5:5, TEV).

Thus, in this living and dramatic parable, Jesus taught us the meaning of *diakonia*. Even as he had said, "I have come to serve and not to be served" (John 10:10), so he brought his teaching to life in a way that the Church was not to forget.

Surely we ought to look upon one another, as Christ showed us, as brothers and sisters, worthy of receiving even a menial task from us. By doing so, we shall surely see the quality of our personal lives being greatly enriched and the warmth of our fellowship being blessed. Jesus tied this teaching together succinctly in his beatitude in John 13:17, "Now that you know these things, you will be blessed if you do them."

CONCLUSION

Jesus came to show us the heart of God. The writer of Hebrews declared of Jesus, "The Son is the radiance of God's glory and the exact representation of his being" (Heb. 1:3). Jesus himself made it clear, "If you knew me, you would know my Father also" (John 8:19). "I and the Father are one" (John 10:30). As T. F. Torrance explains it:

> Thus through the incarnation it is revealed to us that God in His own Being is not closed to us, for He has come to share with us the deepest movement of His divine heart, and so to participate in our human nature that the heart of God beats within it.[37]

The heart of God was revealed in Jesus. The heart of God is love, not static but dynamic, that demonstrates itself in deeds of mercy and kindness. It has as its goal the reconciliation of a lost world.[38] God challenged the sin and evil of the world and conquered in Christ, making possible for humankind the experience of forgiveness and freedom. As we look at Jesus, Torrance says, we see this as one of the distinctive features of his ministry:

> He served God in His mercy and man in his need with the secret of the cross in His heart. . . . Though it was by the Finger or Spirit of God that He brought divine power to bear upon the realm of evil and broke through the thraldom of sin and sickness in miraculous deeds of mercy, He fulfilled His ministry in meekness and lowliness in order to bear the onslaught of evil upon Himself and so to get at the heart of it.[39]

The heart of God was revealed to the Church from the cross of Christ. James Stewart writes, "On the green hill far away they raised the cross, but the real cross was in heaven, in the Father-heart of the eternal."[40] God was in Christ, pouring out his love, pronouncing forgiveness for humankind, which was not able to accomplish such a great salvation for itself.

The key to understanding the heart of God is to experience his forgiveness. This study has attempted to explicate God's forgiveness by looking for the nature of God as taught in the Gospels. God is a loving father who has pronounced forgiveness on his children, who could not find it on their own. His pronouncing forgiveness sets them free to grow and to forgive others.

There is no more powerful dynamic in the world than the realization of a loving and forgiving God. The question that remains for us is how well that message is communicated and translated into life.

Notes

1. F. F. Bruce, *The Message of the New Testament* (Grand Rapids: William B. Eerdmans Publishing Company, 1972), 60.

2. Bruce, p. 57.

3. James G. Emerson, *The Dynamics of Forgiveness* (Philadelphia: The Westminster Press, 1964), 11.

4. Helmut Thielicke, "The Evangelical Faith," in *Theological Foundations for Ministry*, Ray S. Anderson, ed., (Grand Rapids: William B. Eerdmans Publishing Company, 1979), 97.

5. Thielicke, p. 99.

6. Thielicke, p. 107.

7. Joachim Jeremias, *New Testament Theology* (New York: Charles Scribner's Sons, 1971), 230.

8. James S. Stewart, *The Life and Teaching of Jesus Christ* (Richmond, Va.: John Knox Press, n.d.), 81.

9. T. W. Manson, *The Teaching of Jesus* (Cambridge: The University Press, 1970), 91; Deuteronomy 32:6, Isaiah 53:16, Malachi 2:10.

10. Manson, p. 93.

11. Manson, p. 94.

12. James Moffatt, quoted by T. W. Manson, *The Teaching of Jesus*, p. 94.

13. Stewart, *The Life and Teaching of Jesus Christ*, p. 85.

14. George E. Ladd, *A Theology of the New Testament* (Grand Rapids: William B. Eerdmans Publishing Company, 1974), 82.

15. Ladd, pp. 82-90.

16. Ladd, p. 82.

17. Ladd, p. 82.

18. William Barclay, *And Jesus Said* (Philadelphia: The Westminster Press, 1970), 182.

19. Manson, *The Teaching of Jesus*, p. 131.

20. Helmut Thielicke, *The Waiting Father* (New York: Harper and Row Publishers, 1959), 26.

Understanding Forgiveness in the Gospels

21. Stewart, *The Life and Teaching of Jesus Christ*, p. 86.

22. William Barclay, *And Jesus Said*, p. 91.

23. Barclay, p. 86.

24. IV Ezra 8:38ff.

25. Jeremias, *New Testament Theology*, p. 146.

26. Donald Guthrie, *New Testament Theology* (Downers Grove, Ill.: Inter-Varsity Press, 1981), 191-92.

27. Ladd, *A Theology of the New Testament*, p. 88.

28. Thielicke, *The Waiting Father*, p. 26.

29. Harris Franklin Rall, *The Teachings of Jesus* (Nashville: Abingdon Cokesbury Press, 1930), p. 107.

30. Stewart, *The Life and Teaching of Jesus Christ,* p. 96.

31. Manson, *The Teaching of Jesus*, p. 312.

32. J. A. T. Robinson, cited by C. K. Barrett in *The Gospel of John and Judaism*, translated from the German by D. M. Smith (Philadelphia: Fortress Press, 1970), 11-12.

33. Leon Morris, *The Gospel According to John.* The New International Commentary on the New Testament, F .F. Bruce, gen. ed. (Grand Rapids: William B. Eerdmans Publishing Company, 1979), 856.

34. Ernest C. Colwell and Eric Lane Titus, *The Gospel of the Spirit* (New York: Harper and Brothers, 1953), 160.

35. Leon Morris, *The Gospel According to John*, p. 882.

36. Morris, p. 883.

37. Thomas F. Torrance, quoted by Ray S. Anderson, "Living in the World," from *Theological Foundations for Ministry*, Ray S. Anderson, ed., p. 593.

38. Torrance, quoted by Anderson, pp. 717-21.

39. Torrance, quoted by Anderson, p. 725.

40. James S. Stewart, *The Life and Teaching of Jesus Christ*, p. 85.

Faith and Freedom
in Higher Education
Barry L. Callen

In the world of Christian higher education the goal of integrating faith and learning appears to be a constant quest and a perennial problem. If this goal cannot be achieved meaningfully, little is left to justify the separate existence of such a specialized educational enterprise. But if it can be achieved, there is little doubt in the minds of most Christians that something of great significance will have come to pass.

AN IDENTITY CRISIS

Many educators and some church persons assume that a church-related liberal-arts college is an awkward and possibly inconceivable institution of higher education. The very combining of church-related and liberal arts can be seen as a joining of contradictory concepts. Such an institution, by necessity according to the judgment of many, lacks basic educational integrity because the institutional adoption of a particular religious stance is presumed to be in direct opposition to the goals and methods of a classic liberal-arts education.

The credibility of this criticism has been heightened recently as many of these institutions have illustrated the pressures and pitfalls inherent in the religious-liberal arts combination. This has happened when these institutions either have continued to carry such a joint label (even though the reality of institutional life long since has become removed from much that normally is judged to be distinctively Christian) or have so emphasized institutional commitment to a distinctively Christian framework of thought and life that the school may be described best as an *in loco parentis* center of religious indoctrination. In the former case the designation *church-related* has become largely meaningless, while in the latter case the designation *college* has become questionable.

Thus the very future of many institutions traditionally known as church-related liberal-arts colleges is threatened today. This threat grows out of more than their well-publicized financial struggles or the encroachment of the federal govenment on their autonomy. In many cases the root problem is the difficulty they have in discovering a constructive way to relate the Christian faith to the goals of higher education in the midst of a socially and religiously pluralistic culture.

What has proved to be especially elusive is a clear conceptualization of an educational philosophy that is defensible both in terms of Christian theology and educational goals. According to common definitions of *Christian* and *liberal arts*, such a philosophy necessarily would combine emphases on fact and value, commitment and openness, and intellectual freedom in the midst of curricular coherence and creedal assumptions.

Much of the recent history of Protestant church-related colleges in the United States can be viewed in terms of an erosion of many of the traditional meanings of that church relationship. David L. McKenna has described this erosion process as a sequence of changing partners, with such colleges in recent decades shifting their primary relationship from the churches to their alumni, then to accrediting agencies, then to neighboring business communities, and finally to the federal government with its ability to provide financial assistance.[1] The inevitable result of such shifting has been the evolution of a subtle but nonetheless substantial identity crisis for many church-related colleges.

In 1968 Christopher Jencks and David Riesman described the recent history of American higher education in terms of an "academic revolution." They had reference to a development that began with the rise of the research-oriented universities around the turn of this century and was accelerated greatly by the boom in higher education after World War II. This development involved dramatic growth of the public sector. Faculties organized into specialized departments and obtained increasing influence over a large portion of the academic enterprise.

Jencks and Riesman observed that many church-related colleges sought to cope with this academic revolution by simply accepting the prevailing viewpoint of the academic profession about what, how, and whom a college should teach.[2] Charles McCoy highlighted a resultant concern when he concluded that "in seeking to emulate large and often more prestigious public and private institutions, these church-related colleges have not only failed to gain the world but are in the process of losing their own souls."[3]

Apparently church-related liberal-arts colleges now are partially paralyzed by the dilution or at least the diversification of their loyalties and even missions as these are perceived by their multiple constituencies, including faculties trained in secular settings, sponsoring denominations often anxious to perpetuate theological positions, accrediting agencies supervising institutional integrity, and government, business, foundation, and private funding sources with their own standards and agendas.

Wilson L. Thompson also has identified this process

among church-related colleges as one of erosion, of institutional goal displacement resulting from the effects of secularization. His thesis was that such displacement has resulted from a lack of organizational insulation of church-related colleges "from the secularizing influence of their academic task environment," particularly the process of regional accreditation.[4] But however one describes the process or identifies the causes, there is little doubt about the pressure that recent history has been placing on the clarity of the identity of many church-related liberal-arts colleges. The interplay of faith, freedom, and finances has sometimes brought institutional integrity into question.

THE PARADOX OF FREEDOM

Given the growth of the public sector of American higher education and the concurrent processes of changing partners and apparent erosion of the traditional mission of many church-related colleges, it would be helpful to isolate an issue that can function as a means of analysis. What remains of the historic tension in a college that seeks to combine the Christian faith and the liberal arts? Does what remains continue to be faithful both to the religious and educational identities of such institutions?

In recent decades it has been fashionable to think of truth as relative and institutions of higher education as neutral on truth questions. Typically it has been assumed that, with the rise of the scientific method, the popularity of the German university model of higher education, the widespread lessening or ending of sectarian church control of the educational process, and the increasing pluralism of societal values, truth now is rightly in the hands of the questers. The search for truth should proceed in the liberating context of free and original inquiry, not by the required acceptance of some church tradition or the imposition of a supposed divine revelation.

Freedom often has been said to be crucial to the very

process of higher education. One must be free to research, experiment, publish, teach, and learn. Even though freedom necessarily exists in a given setting, and thus tends to be limited by the values and goals of that setting, in higher education it has been argued that freedom must be prominent and pervasive.

A church-related college, therefore, especially one that is serious about its church-relatedness and that also maintains regional accreditation and espouses a liberal arts philosophy of education, appears to be a paradoxical institution. It seeks by definition to embody a harmonious expression of both the Christian and the academic communities. In this context, Robert Parsonage concluded that the "most awkward question arises when a college determines both to seek committed people (in religious terms) and to foster an atmosphere of freedom."[5]

One issue, then, is well-suited as an analytical tool for assessing what appears to be an inherent dilemma for church-related liberal-arts colleges that have achieved regional accreditation and yet have remained serious about the significance of the Christian faith for their educational endeavors. It is the issue of *faculty academic freedom*. This issue was one of the keynotes of the academic revolution and is one that, at least as typically verbalized in the larger academic community, seems at odds with the very nature of a religiously committed institution of higher education.

An institution that is religiously committed would appear to be inherently dual in nature. That circumstance suggests that academic freedom for faculty stands either in an impossible or at least in an awkward position, one often not well understood or appreciated. Professor Arthur Holmes of Wheaton College has spoken of "theistic humanism," a joining of religious commitment and an openness to all avenues of human knowledge and experience, something that was "nourished by the Reformation with its stress on the individual, by Reformed theology with its cultural mandate, and by the sacramental view of nature and human existence which characterizes Catholic, including Anglican thought."[6] But can such a complex and apparently paradoxical stance be translated meaningfully into the very fabric of an institution of higher education? An exploration of the meaning of faculty academic freedom in institutions that seek to embody such a translation should assist in answering this question.

THE LIMITS OF FREEDOM

According to a November 1981 decision of a U. S. Court of Appeals in Atlanta, Georgia, academic freedom does not entitle a college faculty member to refuse to testify in court in regard to his or her previous involvement in a tenure decision. The three-judge panel held that the right to academic freedom is limited by "other important societal goals" and that it "cannot be used to give an institution of higher learning *carte blanche* to practice discrimination."[7] This decision, which appeared to affirm a legitimate and necessary restriction on the academic freedom of faculty members, illustrated a perennial problem area in higher education.

Tension is inevitable when two cherished values collide in such a way that one appears to need sacrificing if the other is to survive. What is to be done, for instance, if the practice of academic freedom results directly in the discrimination of others? The answer of this particular court in Atlanta was to abridge the degree to which academic freedom is actually free. In practice, American history has shown many instances in which the social crises of war, economic depression, and international tension have led to an abridgment of the absoluteness of the freedom implied in the concept of faculty academic freedom.[8]

To change the arena, but not the subject, what about the meaning of academic freedom in a college or university that has officially established for itself the framework in which truth is understood and which has an allegiance to a particular religious community as well as to the academic community? Is the apparent abridgment of the absoluteness of faculty academic freedom in this setting any more severe, any less defensible, any more detrimental to the "liberating" goals of an educational institution than the range of abridgments in public institutions as noted previously?

In the colonial colleges in America, for instance, truth tended to be seen as unitary and was certified by divine revelation. Persons not of "sound doctrine" generally were not acceptable in the classroom. Are similar institutional truth commitments and the questing nature of the contemporary academic enterprise so antithetical to each other that they cannot coexist meaningfully? What about the status of faculty academic freedom in today's colleges that establish the Christian faith as their official truth perspective and simultaneously espouse the traditional goals of a liberal-arts education?

MODELS OF THE PARADOX

After Manning Pattillo and Donald Mackenzie published their major Danforth Commission study on church-sponsored higher education in the United States,[9] reviewer E. M. O'Byrne noted the apparent paradox embedded in the very assumptions of the report, the paradox at the very heart of such colleges. On the one hand, Chapter V argued that "freedom is so basic to the process of teaching and learning that colleges must protect it at all costs." On the other hand, Chapter XII described a "free Christian college" model that was said to be "free because it does not control thought; Christian because it has a definite commitment." The report concluded, and O'Byrne agreed, that

a definite institutional philosophy does not preclude a genuine exposure of the student to alternative views nor prevent free inquiry and expression on the part of the faculty.[10]

Here was an attempt to present a collegiate model that

combined institutional conviction and faculty academic freedom in a way that was seen to be as viable, educationally constructive, and defensible as it appeared to be paradoxical.

Southern Methodist University has provided an example of an institution that has declared itself to be representative of this paradoxical stance. During the years 1960 through 1962 this university engaged in a study of the contemporary meaning and significance of its church relationship. It concluded that church-relatedness was not to be regarded as synonymous with indoctrination, denominationalism, intolerance, or coercion. It saw as unfortunate the fact that the scholarly community for the most part is much more familiar with the sins of the church in this respect than with its virtues."[11] It declared that Southern Methodist University had won "justifiable respect for maintaining a community of free scholarship amidst pressures from numerous sources which seek to coerce and regiment scholarship."[12] But it also declared that a church-related university acknowledges that the mind's adventure "journeys by faith," that church relatedness has a particular definition of truth and a certain view of humankind, and that church relatedness presents a particular interpretation of the meaning of "academic freedom."[13]

Anderson College, Anderson, Indiana, presented a more recent example. After a year of intense self-examination prompted in part by questions from some persons within its sponsoring church constituency, the college published its own view of the nature of its partnership with the church. It stated that its

> curricular design and community life combine the honesty and rigor of academic inquiry and the perspectives and mission emerging from Biblical revelation. It lives in an atmosphere of free inquiry, even while it affirms that all knowledge is understood most fully in the light of God's redemptive activity in Jesus Christ as that is interpreted through the historic witness of the Bible and the contemporary ministry of the Holy Spirit.[14]

These two examples help to clarify the nature of an

apparent paradox that lies at the very heart of many church-related colleges and universities. The concept of faculty academic freedom is both championed in principle and qualified in practice. There appears to be an inherent tension in the intellectual style of such institutions, with the presence of the free questing of the traditional scholarly life on the one hand and, on the other, the institutional acceptance of a pattern of revealed absolutes within which the questing proceeds.

So the central question remains: Can the presence of such a tension constitute a genuine educational community in which faculty academic freedom has meaning or is it merely an invitation to an intolerable intellectual schizophrenia?

RECENT RESEARCH

Seldom has research among church-related colleges in recent years singled out the issue of faculty academic freedom for particular attention. This fact, added to the obvious variety of commitments and emphases among church-related colleges, has made it difficult at best to draw dependable generalizations. Even so, especially in colleges that both espouse a liberal-arts philosophy and take very seriously their institutional religious commitments, faculty academic freedom has tended to be pictured paradoxically. It has been seen as something to be desired and yet something to be tempered by the Christian perspective to which the institution and its church constituency are committed. Whatever else they desire to be, apparently most such institutions intend to be *educational* rather than *religious-indoctrination* institutions; and the available information tends to affirm that, such a vision, awkward and delicate as it is, has been durable and viable to a significant degree.

It is noteworthy that many of the institutional members of the Christian College Coalition specifically affirm the 1940 "Statement of Principles on Academic Freedom and Tenure" of the American Association of University Professors.[15]

They assume that the freedom to pursue truth openly and honestly, although responsibly and respectfully, is not contrary to the spirit of Christian faith and is not necessarily a danger to the maintenance of that faith within a religiously committed academic community. In fact, according to the faculty handbook of Northwestern College, Orange City, Iowa, "the Christian faith is a liberating force in human affairs and a remarkably good base for an education in the liberal arts."

Both the paradox and the religious and educational idealism within that paradox remain. In the words of the faculty handbook of Westmont College (Santa Barbara, California), "within the framework of the Articles of Faith, the faculty member of Westmont College enjoys the utmost freeodm." Original research and ancient revelation are seen as comrades, not competitors.

Faith and freedom may indeed be in tension as the process of higher education moves forward, but experience has shown that the tension can be healthy and productive. May it be so!

Notes

1. David L. McKenna, "Changing Partnerships in Christian Higher Education," *Christianity Today* XIV:23, 5-7.

2. Christopher Jencks and David Riesman, *The Academic Revolution* (Chicago: University of Chicago Press, 1977), 322.

3. Charles McCoy, *The Responsible Campus* (Nashville: Board of Education, United Methodist Church, 1972), 19.

4. Wilson L. Thompson, *Small Colleges and Goal Displacement; A Study of Christian College Secularization* (University of Oregon Ph.D. dissertation, 1978), 25.

5. Robert Parsonage, ed., *Church Related Higher Education* (Valley Forge, PA: Judson Press, 1979), 80-81.

Faith and Freedom in Higher Education

6. As quoted by J. Richard Chase, Inaugural Address, Wheaton College, September 17, 1982, p. 9.

7. *The Chronicle of Higher Education* 23:13, November 25, 1981, p. 1. The issue of June 16, 1983 reported that the Supreme Court refused to review this contempt-of-court conviction of a University of Georgia professor who went to jail rather than reveal how he had voted in a tenure case.

8. See John Brubacher and Willis Rudy, *Higher Education in Transition* (New York: Harper & Row, 1976), pp. 322-29.

9. Manning Pattillo, Jr. and Donald Mackenzie, *Church-Sponsored Higher Education in the United States* (Washington, D.C., American Council on Education, 1966).

10. E. M. O'Byrne, *et al.*, "Can the Churches Take Their Educational Responsibilities Seriously?" *Journal of Higher Education* 39:3, March 1968, 173-75.

11. George A. Buttrick, *et al.*, "Toward a Philosophy of the Church-Related University," *The Christian Scholar*, Summer 1962, 92.

12. Buttrick, *et al.*, p. 91.

13. Buttrick, *et al.*, pp. 93-95.

14. *Anderson College: In Partnership with the Church*, Institutional brochure published by Anderson College, Fall 1981.

15. Examples: Biola University, North Park College, Olivet Nazarene College, Seattle Pacific University, and Westmont College.

The Christian Community
and Its Ministry
Douglas E. Welch

INTRODUCTION

In seeking to understand what may be called Karl Barth's theology of mission[1] we must of necessity work from within the wider context of his ecclesiology. To Barth one cannot speak seriously about the community of Christ without reference to its essential missionary nature. The Church is Christ's body, "His own earthly-historical form of existence" (IV. 3.681).[2] He sends it among all peoples as his own people, "ordained for its part to confess Him before all men, to call them to Him" (IV. 3.681). Thus, to speak of the Church is to speak not of an institution, but of a living community sent by the Holy Spirit to make known to the whole world the joyous news of God's reconciling event in Jesus Christ. To assume that because Barth devotes only four and a half pages to foreign missions he therefore has an inadequate theology of mission is to misunderstand the missiological dimensions of his ecclesiology.[3]

In this study we shall endeavor to examine Barth's own

views on the mission of the Church. In order to do this effectively, it is necessary first of all to deal with his understanding of the *nature* of the community of Christ. What kind of community is it that Christ calls into existence and sends into the world? Certainly the nature of the community has a direct relationship to its function, its mission.

This is not to say that the community determines the mission, for the mission is predetermined in the Christ event. It is to say that the nature of the mission cannot be considered as though it were something quite apart from the nature of the community called into existence by the Holy Spirit for that mission. In other words, to speak of mission one must speak of Christ's community. And to speak of Christ's community one must speak of mission. By dealing first with the nature of the community and then with the nature of its ministry we are not suggesting two clearly demarcated aspects of ecclesiology. Indeed, they comprise a single theme. But for ease of analysis we will deal first with one, and then with the other.

JESUS AND HIS COMMUNITY

The vocation of the human race according to Barth, is to be Christian (IV. 3.554). As a Christian, a person is a witness of Jesus Christ. This is his or her call, or *klēsis*. But *klēsis* must lead unavoidably to *ekklesia* or community (IV. 3.681). One is not a witness in isolation, or a Christian in isolation. Indeed, as Barth states, the "vocation to be a Christian means vocation or calling into Christendom or the Church, i.e., into the living community of the living Lord Jesus Christ" (IV. 3.681). One is not first called to be a Christian, and then called into the Church, or vice versa. The call to be a Christian is a call to enter a community, a community of witnesses. They are simultaneous occurrences. One cannot be found without the other.

To be sure, as Barth acknowledges, no passage in the Gospels refers directly to the establishment of the *ekklesia*

Ministry in the Thought of Karl Barth

(cf.IV. 3.683ff). But does this mean that Jesus established no such community? It does not. He states that the establishment of the community could not be "a definite and distinctive event in the Gospel tradition." It was rather a necessary part of the Jesus-event. Thus, says Barth, "The whole of the Gospel narrative as an account of Jesus" was at the same time "an account of the birth of the Christian community, a development of the people of God . . . of the last time." This is evident in the calling of the Twelve, the mission of the Seventy, the Beautitudes, the institution of the Lord's Supper, the Great Commission, and the outpouring of the Spirit at Pentecost. Barth concludes,

> Indeed, do we not have to go further and say that the whole Gospel record at least from the baptism of Jesus . . . to the story of Pentecost is implicitly also an account of the origin of this people, of its beginning in the words and acts of Jesus, of its gathering, maintaining, upbuilding, ordering and sending by Him? . . . Everywhere, as we are forced to say, the texts themselves speak of a Jesus who founds His community and of the community founded by Him. And it is for this very reason that there can be no special account of this foundation (IV. 3.684).

The call to be a Christian, then, must be seen also as Christ's call to become part of a community, a sent community, an extension in the world of God's witness in and through Christ.

A SPECIAL COMMUNITY

This leads us to the first characteristic of the Christian community: it is a special community, a distinct community, an elect community, the people of God of the last time. It is the community of Christ. It is called into existence by him. "He is the man," Barth declares, "in whose person God has, of course, elected and loved from all eternity the wider circle of humanity as a whole, but also, with a view to this wider circle, the narrower circle of a special race, of His own community within humanity" (IV. 3.682) Persons are called to be Christians, and by virtue of that fact, to be disciples and witnesses. They are constituted a special people, "always with a view to all humanity." They do not so constitute themselves.

Barth is very careful to stress the fact that the community exists by virtue of Christ's calling. It is called into existence by Christ. It is maintained in existence by Christ. It is the community of his witnesses, "bound, engaged, and committed to Him" (IV. 3.752). He is its Lord. It exists only in him, only as it "belongs to Him, listens to Him, and is obedient to Him. It exists only in union with Him, as the branches exist only in union with the vine" (IV. 3.753). It does not live by its own effort or activity, or by its own faith, love, and hope. It lives only as Christ lives. The being of the community is a "predicate or dimension of the being of Jesus Christ Himself" (IV. 3.754). But as it lives in him it shares in his power, his holiness, his freedom, his victory.

A VISIBLE COMMUNITY

Not only is it a special community, *Christ's* community, it is also a *visible* community. It is not a mystical, invisible, other-worldly community without form or structure. It is a visible, historical entity. It exists in world-occurrence. As Barth writes, "The community which was created and lives by this Word, the people of Jesus Christ, also exists in the flesh . . . within world-occurrence" (IV. 3.723). In other words, the Christian community is a part of historical reality. Barth continues,

And we must be more precise and say that it does not do so like an embedded foreign body, like a meteorite which has fallen from a distant sphere or a pearl in its shell, but as itself a genuinely and thoroughly worldly element participating in world-occurrence. There is an ecclesiological as well as a christological Docetism which we must carefully avoid at this point. The Christian community does not merely resemble the other elements, magnitudes and factors in world-occurrence; for all the particularity of its structure and situation it is of like manner with them. It does not hover over them; it exists on the same level. It can thus be seen together with them, and critically and constructively compared with them. It is itself a people like so many others (IV. 3.723).

Thus the community of Christ cannot be socially or culturally monolithic. In the first place it does not have any, in his words, "intrinsically and absolutely distinctive social form." From the very beginning "its constitution and order have been broadly determined and conditioned by political, economic, and cultural models more or less imperatively forced on it by its situation in world history" (IV. 3.739). The Christ community possesses no intrinsically sacred sociology or language. Like other peoples it exists in a specified cultural setting. It is even possible to say that the given cultural model of a specific people is also the model of the people of God among them. They may march to a different drumbeat, but they do it as participants in human cultures. In other words, the community of Christ within a culture will in very many respects look like any other community within the same culture.

It is of very great importance to a theology of mission to conceive of the community of Christ as a community within world-occurrence in this manner. An "embedded foreign body," an alien transplant, within a culture is a distortion of the Christ community. The true community is at once visible and culturally relevant. As a special community of Christ it is not bound by cultural forms, but at the same time it cannot be entirely free from them. It may exist in any sociological form, but it cannot exist without sociological form (cf. IV. 3.740ff.)

AN INVISIBLE COMMUNITY

But, Barth hastens to add, the community of Christ, while highly and specifically and necessarily visible, must at the same time possess the characteristic of invisibility. While it is totally *dependent* on its environment, it is also totally *free* in

145

relation to it (IV. 3.734). While it is *a* people, it is also *this* people. "Like Israel in the Old Testament," so Barth asserts, "the Christian community is not just a people in world-occurrence but this people. It is just as essential to it to be this people as to be a people. And it is just as essential to it to be not merely visible as one people among many but also invisible as this people." (IV. 3.726). Since it is the community of Christ "this" people is "totally and properly both visible, i.e., fully human and invisible, i.e., fully God (IV. 3.726). To view the Christ community as less than this is to become involved in an unacceptable ecclesiological Docetism. We must view it, according to Barth, as being both fully world-occurring and world-transcending (cf. IV. 3.724).

As world-occurring the community of Christ is universal; as world-transcending it is particular. The characteristic of invisibility, then, speaks of that particularity. As this particular people, the community is wholly unique and distinct. Barth writes,

> Just as it is one among others in that it is wholly *ad extra* and like all the other elements, magnitudes and factors in world-occurrence, so it is this particular people in that it is from within and unlike all others. Nor does this mean that it is unlike only as one example in a species, or one species in a genus, or one genus in a class. It means that it is unlike because it is unique and incomparable, an example, a species, a genus, a class apart (IV. 3.727).

For this reason, Barth concludes, Christianity cannot be considered on the same plane as other religions. It cannot be conceived in historico-critical terms as some mere "link in historical development." It cannot because it has an essential invisibility, a withinness, that makes it quite unlike any other element in world-occurrence, such as Islam or Buddhism. Any interpretation, therefore, based only on the visibility of the community, is erroneous. To fail to see its true invisibility is to misunderstand its total being, Barth states, "including that wherein it is visible."

Ministry in the Thought of Karl Barth

The characteristic of invisibility speaks also of the alien nature of the community of Christ. While it has a place in world-occurrence, it is not a place that belongs to it self-evidently. "It cannot be said of it," Barth asserts, "as of the estate, or work, or trade, or the different forms of culture, that it belongs to the essential constants of human existence and therefore world-occurrence" (IV. 3.743). It is, in inward essence, a community that does not really belong. Its existence in world-occurrence is a marginal existence. It is a pilgrim people, a homeless people, of essentially alien status (cf. IV. 3.744ff). It cannot settle down, then, simply to play the role of "a competing secular construct" within society. To be sure, Barth concedes, it exists in world-occurrence. In its outwardness, its visibility, it is secular in form and speech, i.e., it is culturally shaped and colored. However, for

> all its dependence on the world and world-occurrence, it cannot be ruled and determined by these. The wonderful freedom with which it may assemble itself from all human societies and across all their frontiers, and with which its members, i.e., Christians, are commanded and permitted to exist also as members of these societies, must always show itself in the fact that no matter where these Christians may be, or what else they may be, they mut always see themselves and act first and decisively as Christians, and only then as members of this or that nation, citizens of this or that state, participants in the work of this or that cultural or other society (IV. 3.741).

A COMMISSIONED COMMUNITY

And then finally, the community of Christ is a commissioned community, a "sent" community. We have alluded to this in several places in the previous material. Barth is quite unequivocal at this point. This community has been called into existence by Christ and sent into the world as a witness of Christ to call peoples to him (cf. IV. 3.681). The Christ community does not exist for itself, but for Christ and the world. "The true community of Jesus Christ," Barth writes, "is the community which God has sent out into the world in and with its foundation. As such it exists for the world." And this, not because of any dignity, authority, or power inherent within the community itself, but by virtue of the fact that it is "invested with dignity, authority, and power by Christ," and only "in the context of His divine sending" (IV. 3.768).

Barth sees the sending of Christ into the world and the sending of the Church into the world as comparable sendings. They have the same *origin*: "The one God who sends Him as the Father also sends them through Him the Son." And they have the same *goal*: "He and they are both sent into the world, which means very generally that they are directed to the world and exist for it" (IV. 3.768). The sending of the Christ community, then, is an extension of the sending of Christ by the Father (John 17:18; 20:21). The mission to the world that Christ began is the mission that his community continues. The community exists for that purpose, and for no other. As Christ's community it exists for the world, not for itself. Barth writes of this in a lengthy paragraph, which we shall quote in part:

> Where the life of the Church is exhausted in self-serving it smacks of death; the decisive thing has been forgotten, that this whole life is lived only in the exercise of what we call the Church's service as ambassador, proclamation, *kerygma*. A Church that recognizes its commission will neither desire to nor be able to petrify in any of its functions, to be the Church for its own sake. There is the "Christ believing group"; but this group is *sent out*; "Go and preach the Gospel!" It does not say, "Go and celebrate services!" "Go and edify yourselves with the sermon!" "Go and celebrate the sacraments!" "Go and present yourselves in a liturgy!" "Go and devise a theology which may gloriously unfold like the *Summa* of St. Thomas!" Of course, there is nothing to forbid all this; there may exist very good cause to do it all; but nothing, nothing at all for its own sake! In it all the one thing must prevail: "Proclaim the gospel to every creature!" The Church runs like a herald to deliver the message. It is

148

Ministry in the Thought of Karl Barth

not a snail that carries its little house on its back and is so
well off in it, that only now and then it sticks out its feelers,
and then thinks that the "claim of publicity" has been
satisfied. No, the Church lives by its commission as herald.
. . . Where the Church is living, it must ask itself whether it
is serving this commission or whether it is a purpose in itself?
If the second is the case, then as a rule it begins to smack of
the "sacred," to affect piety, to play the priest and to
mumble. Anyone with a keen nose will smell it and find it
dreadful! Christianity is not sacred; rather there breathes in
it the fresh air of the Spirit. Otherwise it is not Christianity.
For it is an out-and-out "worldly" thing open to all humanity:
"Go into all the world and proclaim the Gospel to every
creature" (1959: 146ff).

This going, according to Barth, is to be a confident going.
Christ's community is not to concern itself with success or
failure. "It does not," he insists, "need to compare, equate or
confuse its work with that of others directed to merely
provisional and limited ends." It should rather hold its head
high and maintain its direction. In doing so is its sustenance
and strength to be found. "It has simply to do what it has
been commissioned and commanded to do," not concerning
itself with the outcome (IV. 3.750).

THE COMMUNITY AND ITS MINISTRY

Barth has a great deal more to say about the nature of the
Christ community. We have been able to touch only a
sufficient number of the high points to enable us to trace the
general outline of his ecclesiology. This has been necessary,
as we stated earlier, because in Barth's ecclesiology we find
the *immediate* roots of this theology of mission. The community of Christ, we have concluded, Barth views as a very
special, unique, incomparable community called by Christ
into existence in world-occurrence, not to exist for itself, but
for the world. In its outwardness it becomes a part of the
milieu in which it exists. But inwardly it stands apart,
existing on the fringe of world-occurrence, characterized by

homelessness and foreignness. As Christ was in the world so is his community. As God sent Christ into the world, so Christ sends his elect community. In it he speaks his word by the power of the Holy Spirit. And through it he speaks to the world.

With this in mind, we turn then to seek a fuller understanding of Barth's views of the ministry for which the Christian community has been called into existence. Here we face somewhat of a semantic problem. Barth appears to designate the reason for the calling into existence of the community *generally* as its "task," and *specifically* as its "ministry." Under other circumstances the word *mission* could be made to include both. But Barth used the word *mission* only of a very specific aspect of ministry. Therefore we shall broaden his use of *ministry* to include both general and specific aspects, recognizing that the *task*—which we may call *mission*—provides the boundaries of the *ministry*—in which we may include *missions*.

The Basic Task

The Christian community is a sent community. But it is not, according to Barth, sent into the world "haphazardly or at random, but with a very definite task." It does not come into existence and then only later acquire its task. Neither does it exist apart from its task, says Barth, "so that there can be no question whether or not it might have to execute it" (IV. 3.795). Barth concludes,

> Its task constitutes and fashions it from the very outset. If it had not been given it, it would not have come into being. If it were to lose it, it would not continue. It is not, then, a kind of imparted dignity. It exists only as it has it, or rather only as the task has it. Nor is it a kind of burden laid upon it. It is the inalienable foundation which bears it. Every moment of its history it is measured by it. It stands or falls with it in all its expressions, in all its actions or abstention. It either understands itself in the light of its task or not at all . . . The Christian community lives by and with its task (IV. 3.796).

Ministry in the Thought of Karl Barth

And what is that task? In a word, *witness.* The simplest and most biblical formation of the task, so Barth believes, is found in Acts 1:8: "And you shall bear witness for me." (NEB). It is a task defined and delimited by the uniqueness of the person, work, and name of Jesus Christ (IV. 3.797). Thus it is not only a witness *for* Jesus, but a witness *of* Jesus, a witness that God was in him reconciling the world. It is attestation to "a great and comprehensive affirmation," a Divine Yes, which is Jesus Christ. We do not, Barth declares, "point beyond Him or speak of something distinct from Him, but . . . point to Him." And so it is that Christ himself is the "content" of witness (IV. 3.797). The content of the witness is the gospel, "the good, glad tidings of Jesus Christ, of the real act and true revelation" of incarnation (IV. 3.800).

Or stated yet another way, the task of the community of Christ is the declaration, explication, and application of the gospel. The community receives the gospel, Barth declares, in order to pass it on to other people. "It can only acquaint them with it." It is not the task of the community to cause the world to believe and know the gospel. That can only be the work of Jesus Christ himself through the Holy Spirit (IV. 3.844).

But *proclamation* in and of itself is not sufficient. There must also be *explication*, or explanation. In other words, the gospel must be made "intelligible" (IV. 3.846). "The world," Barth writes, "has need that the gospel should be explained to it as it is declared" (IV. 3.847). By explaining the gospel he means "to narrate the history which God himself has inaugurated, which He rules, in which He has taken the world and man to Himself, and in which man finds himself taken up into intercourse and fellowship with Him" (IV. 3.849). To explain the gospel is to "expound, unfold, and articulate its content" in order to make it perceptible and intelligible to the world. It is not to make it knowable, for only God can do that through his Spirit (IV. 3.850).

151

And finally, there must be *application* of the gospel. In other words, there must be proclamation and explanation as "evangelical address." The gospel must be directly addressed to persons of the world, summoning them to faith, not speaking past them or over them, but directly to them (IV.1 3.850). It must call people to true knowledge "by at least giving an indirect push in the direction of salvation and peace" (IV. 3.851ff). "To address men evangelically," Barth concludes, "is decisively to present to them . . . the Gospel in such a way that they come to see its crucial application to them, that so far as any human word can do so it pricks their hearts . . . that it brings them to realize that the reference is to them." (IV. 3.852ff).

And one final question: who is to be addressed in the task of proclamation or witness? To Barth the answer is very simple and straightforward: "The man who lacks the knowledge of the Gospel and is thus supremely needy" (IV. 3.806). That person may be an adult or a child, male or female, eastern or western, European or African, civilized, half-civilized, or uncivilized, a person of any political and economic context, a person who is "immediate to God, and therefore to his neighbour." There is no one, Barth concludes, to whom the Christ community "has not to turn in the discharge of its task, just as there is no man who in his particular situation, determined on every hand, is not immediate to God and his neighbour" (IV. 3.804). In short, those who are to be evangelically addressed are all who are on the other side of "the frontier which separates non-Christian humanity" from the community of Jesus Christ (cf. IV. 3.853).

SPEECH-ACTION WITHIN THE COMMUNITY

With that we turn to specific aspects of the ministry of the Christian community. Ministry, according to Barth, is to be defined in terms of speech-action. He sees in "the active life of Jesus" a differentiation (not division) of ministry "into speech which is also action on the one side, and action which is also speech on the other" (IV. 3.862). The ministry of the church, then, is to be performed as verbal speech, which is action. "If we ever come cross a form of the Church's ministry," Barth contends, "in which there is neither speech on the one side nor action on the other, it may be affirmed with certainty that at least this is not a basic form" (IV. 3.864).

The first kind of speech-action dealt with by Barth is that which takes place within the Christian community. It is basically speech-action through which the Holy Spirit is able to upbuild the community. The basic task of the community is witness to the world, that is, ministry *ad extra*—which may also be referred to as mission. But there is also a necessary dimension of ministry that is *ad intra*. The community, Barth states, must hold both dimensions in meaningful tension:

> It stands in the service of those who in fact live in the world without God and their fellows, and therefore in forfeiture of their own true selves. To such it is sent. When active in the field it is what it truly is. Yet its resolute outward service has necessarily an inner dimension. Its witness must also be addressed to its own members and continually made perceptible to them. None of the Christians united in it so shares in its knowledge and confession that he does not need every day to be enlightened and awakened fresh to this participation, and therefore nourished, comforted and admonished as a living Christian. The same Word which the community has to attest to the world will and must be continually heard afresh by it to its own constant gathering, upbuilding and sending. . . . Christians can obviously be serviceable in the ministry of the Word to those without only if they find themselves constantly placed under the same Word (IV. 3.832).

The danger, however, is that the ministry *ad intra*, that is, speech-action within the community intended for the upbuilding and continual renewal of the community, may become an end in itself. The only ways this can be avoided is for the community to keep continually before itself the awareness that its basic commitment must be to ministry *ad extra*. "If its inward service," Barth concludes, "is not to become an institution for private satisfaction in concert, or a work of sterile inbreeding, it must accept the priority of its sending to the world, or its task in relation to those who are without" (IV. 3.833). The Christian community, then, is first and foremost a "missionary community." But if it is to be also an "authentic Christian community," willing and able to carry out its missionary task, it must be continually renewed from within by the power of the Holy Spirit through the Word (cf.IV. 3.833).

Speech-action—which may be acting by speaking, or speaking by acting—within the community will include *divine service* as praise to God (IV. 3.865ff); explicit *proclamation* of the gospel, proclamation that "summons, invites, and commands," rather than disputes or instructs academically (IV. 3.869); catechetical *instruction* (IV. 3.870ff); the ministry of *theology* as an "integrating element" in the ministry of the community (IV. 3.879ff); *prayer*, not only as an individual exercise, but as "a movement in which Christians jointly and persistently engage" (IV. 3.882ff); the *cure of souls* through pastoral care, Church discipline, and so forth (IV. 3.885ff); *exemplary Christian living* (IV. 3.887ff); *Christian service*, i. e., the exercise of the diaconate, witnessing through caring for the needy both within and outside of the community (IV. 3.889ff); *prophetic action*, in which the community interprets its own history and future in such a way that self-examination and self-amendment are constant (IV. 3.895ff); and the establishment of *Christian fellowship*, especially through baptism and the Lord's Supper (IV. 3.898ff). The first four of these basic aspects of ministry, according to Barth, are primarily speech; those that follow, primarily action. But each partakes of the other. And both build up the Church for ministry *ad extra*, that is, ministry beyond its own borders.

Ministry in the Thought of Karl Barth

The second kind of speech-action, then, is specifically that kind of speech-action engaged in by the community of Christ in its witness to the world. Barth deals first of all with the task which is "excellently summed up in the term 'evangelization' " (IV. 3.872). It is legitimate, he believes, to distinguish evangelization from missions and "what we now call home missions." It refers primarily to evangelical address directed to "those who stand in the more immediate environs of the community" (IV. 3.872). And who are they? They are those who, on the basis of "the curious notion of *corpus christianum*" and "the even more curious custom of infant baptism,"

> seem to belong to the community and yet do not really belong to it to the extent that they have no obvious part in either the knowledge or the resultant ministry of the community. They are thus men who, being "Christians" before they know what is at issue or have made any resolve or expressed any desire to be such, are just as much strangers to the Gospel, or have only the same hearsay knowledge, as if they belonged to the heathen races to whom the disciples are sent (IV. 3.872).

Evangelization, then, is directed specifically to "non-Christian Christendom." It is a ministry of proclamation and teaching intended to win those who ought to be Christians, but are not. In other words, is is speech-action designed to awaken to the knowledge of God through Jesus Christ "the lost sheep of the house of Israel"—the nominal Christian. Barth speaks directly of this when he says, "The concern of evangelization is precisely to sound out the Gospel on this shifting frontier between true and merely nominal Christians" (IV. 3.873). Evangelization aims at bringing such people to belief and obedience, to becoming in practice what they are in theory. A Church not engaged in this ministry, Barth declares, is "either not yet or no longer the Church, or only a dead Church, itself standing in supreme need or

155

renewal by evangelization" (IV. 3.873).

But apostolic speech-action also includes *mission*. This, according to Barth, is "mission in the narrower sense, which is also the true and original sense, in which sending or sending out to the nations to attest the gospel is the very root of the existense and therefore of the whole ministry of the community" (IV. 3.874). The community of Christ, as we have seen, is a commissioned community, a sent community, a community with a specific vocation to "proclaim the Gospel to every creature," to "make disciples of all nations." It is by its very constitution and nature a missionary community. Not only must it therefore engage in evangelization of the nominal-Christian world, but also in missions to the non-Christian world. As Barth concludes, "The vocation which constitutes the community is directly the command to take this message to this world, to the nations or the 'heathen.' As it is obedient to this command, it engages in foreign missions" (IV. 3.874).

Barth then proceeds to a more explicit discussion of "foreign missions." In the first place, they are predicated on the conviction that Christ died and rose again "for these heathen too." All that is necessary for the salvation of all has been accomplished in the Christ-event. The task of missions, therefore, "can only consist in announcing this to them" (IV. 3.874). By "announcing," of course, Barth has in mind far more than mere declaration of the gospel. As we noted earlier, it is the task of the Christian community not only to *declare* the gospel, but to *explain* it in order that comprehension might take place through the direct ministry of the Holy Spirit, and to *apply* it through evangelical speech, i. e., to appeal for a verdict. Barth was not one who would have had any time for the "Gospel blimp" approach. Mere declaration is a parody of the community's task.

Second, the entire community is "the acting subject" in foreign missions. If it is not, then it is not in reality the community of Christ (IV. 3.875). Barth is not here suggesting that the community is itself a missionary "society." There may be, in practice, he says, "definite circles or unions or societies which initiate missions" (IV. 3.875). It is important that we endeavor to understand Barth here, for he is often misinterpreted at this point. The essential unity of the community, he insists, does not imply uniformity (cf.IV. 3.855). The Christian community "cannot be a barracks, nor can its members be uniformed inhabitants, nor can their activity be the execution of a well-drilled manoeuvre" (IV. 3.875). The ministry of the community will inevitably, under the Holy Spirit, display an "integrated multiplicity." Barth concludes,

This implies that the "communion of the Holy Ghost" (2 Cor. 13.13) which constitutes the whole community, in which alone individuals can seriously participate in its ministry and witness and from which they cannot in any circumstances separate themselves, will always express itself concretely in the form of specific communions which within the sphere of the one action of the community are called and equipped in detail for the same or similar action. *It can and should develop special working fellowships to which all Christians cannot and will not necessarily belong but in which, in execution of the activity demanded of all Christians, a particular service is rendered in common in a particular form of thought, speech and action, Christian witness being given in a particular way* (IV.3.856, italics mine. Cf. also IV. 3.857ff).

What Barth seems to be saying here is that while there are no ministries within the community that are not the ministries of the *entire* community, specialized ministries are in fact committed to "specialized working fellowships," which act on behalf of the entire community. Such fellowships cannot function as if they were no longer part of the community. Their work cannot be considered their special preserve that excludes the community. "The rest of the community," Barth asserts, "is not to be released even in appearance from the missionary obligation laid upon it in its totality. The missionary society can only act representatively for the whole community which is as such a missionary community" (IV. 3.875). Barth's concern is not to deny the validity of specialized fellowships concerned with home and foreign missions, but rather his concern is the existence within the community of the attitude that foreign missions are not a legitimate concern of the entire community. He would further, perhaps, deny the validity of the activities of fellowships that in effect prevent the participation of the full community. This is not an argument favoring only *denominational* mission societies. Under those circumstances they may well cross denominational boundaries. But they should not be exclusive or schismatic, or lead to the founding of sects that disrupt, rather than express, the "communion of the Holy Ghost" (cf. IV. 3.856).

Third, the only purpose of missions must be the proclamation, or the making known, of the gospel to "foreign peoples." The motivating force behind Christian missions must be the desire to glorify God and bring others to the light of the knowledge of salvation. Missions are illegitimate if the aim is to "strengthen confessional positions," or "extend European or American culture and civilization," or to "propagate one of the modes of thought and life familiar and dear to the older Christian world be reason of its antiquity," or to "support colonial or general political interests and aspirations" (IV. 3.875). The paramount concern in missions must be the enlightenment and conversion of the "heathen."[4]

Fourth, missions in their relations with non-Christian religions must be governed by two presuppositions: (1) that such religions will be "valued and taken seriously," rather than be treated with arrogance and disrespect; and (2) that taking them seriously and treating them with respect will not mean any compromise of the "radical uniqueness" of the gospel. So while a "sincere respect is needed, there must at the same time be an "equally sincere lack of repect" for the "so-called" religions (IV. 3.875). Barth would obviously see no point to dialogue with non-Christian religions *as a philosophy*.

Ministry in the Thought of Karl Barth

Fifth, missions must be concerned to establish "the whole ministry" of the community. They must include preaching, instruction, prayer, fellowship, evangelization, and diaconate. This will necessitate both educational and medical missions "in many places if not universally, and in the early stages if not permanently" (IV. 3.875). But, Barth hastens to add, "These tasks cannot become an end in themselves, so that missions cannot be conducted solely along the lines of the work of Albert Schweitzer" (IV. 3.876). There should be no regrets, Barth continues, when such tasks are taken out of the hands of missions, "since this enables them to apply themselves with greater concentration of energy to their proper work" (IV. 3.876).

Sixth, the goal of missions is not to convert heathen. Rather, this is the work of God through the Holy Spirit. Hence, Barth asserts, "The goal of the missionary work of the community must be to attest to the heathen the work and Word of the God who, as He has created them by His call, wills to make them, too, His witnesses, and to equip them as such" (IV. 3.876). Like John the Baptizer, the community summons the "heathen" to readiness for the knowledge of the mightier One who comes after, to readiness for the baptism of the Spirit and thus for faith and obedience" (IV. 3.854). The community must not forget its role as forerunner, or its dependence on the Holy Spirit. Nor must it forget that it is God who calls the heathen and equips them for witness, as he wills, and in ways he chooses. The community must be prepared to recognize this calling and equipping, even though it may be on a somewhat different level from its own.

And then, finally, missionary work must take the form of serving, not mastering and ruling, and this from the very beginning. Its purpose is to "lead the heathen themselves to become witnesses, to become the community, by the awakening call of God' (IV. 3.876). The mission is not to consider itself as being above the community, according to Barth, but should become a part of it, "advising and helping on the grounds of its longer experience." At the point the "new community" can do without the mission, the mission must "hand over the missionary task to the new and young and native community" (IV. 3.876). The real purpose of missions to the heathen, then, is to raise up missionary communities among the heathen, and so make themselves "superfluous."

CONCLUSION

One could say a great deal more concerning Barth's theology of mission—which is in essence a theology of the Church. But this is sufficient to demonstrate our thesis, namely, that Barth cannot, in reality, be accused of a truncated theology of mission. It is not here being suggested that we must, or indeed can, agree with all Barth has to say on the subject. But we can at least agree that Barth presents a very full-orbed and biblically based ecclesiology that insists on the essential missionary nature of the community of Christ. It is not a closed community, but a community for the world; not a politically powerful and ruling community, but an alien and serving community. It is a called and sent community, able to exist in any society or culture as a part of it, and yet apart from it. The very nature of the community as constituted by God through Jesus Christ is such that it can continue to live as the community of Christ only as it engages resolutely and unceasingly in its task of witness to all peoples not yet a part of the new covenant community.

This is a biblical view, and one that needs to be clearly heard today. The community of Christ was conceived in and for mission. Its ministry *ad intra* is not to become an end in itself—as it obviously has in far too many instances. It is to be so nurtured and upbuilt by the Holy Spirit through the Word that it becomes both a disruptive and a transforming presence in human societies. And beyond this, the community needs to hear again Barth's insistent word that all that it does must result in persons' being unmistakably summoned to repentance and conversion to Christ. Barth would never agree with modern conciliar theologies of mission that are content with Christian presence, or Christian dialogue, or political and economic liberation *as ends in themselves*. The community that has no other goals than these is a community that itself stands in need of evangelization and renewal.

Notes

1. In this study we are concerned simply to understand what Barth has to say about the nature of the church and its mission in the world. The aim is to set forth his theology of mission, not to provide a critique of it. Since Barth's ecclesiology, or Theology of the Church, has so greatly influenced missiological thought, knowing what he is saying and why he is saying it is important. No effort is made here either to espouse his viewpoint, or to oppose it.

2. The source material for this study is drawn from Barth's *Church Dogmatics.* The appropriate volume containing the material in question is Volume IV, Part 3, Second Half, *The Doctrine of Reconciliation*—hereafter referred to simply as IV. 3. and page number. Since this is a presentation of Barth's views, his writing is quoted freely.

3. A colleague in the field of missiology remarked that Barth "casually dismisses missions with a mere four pages out of thousands." That remark has triggered this study. (The word *missiology* is here being used in the modern sense—as defined by Orlando Costas in *Theology of the Crossroads in Contemporary Latin America*—of "critical reflection in missionary praxis," or the study of "The church's life in mission" (p. 18) Missiology is a new and emerging academic discipline, but it is also the Church in mission reflecting critically on its own theory and practice, evaluating, correcting, developing new models in the light of biblical theology, history, social science, and communication theory.)

4. The term *heathen* is not a missiologically acceptable

term today. It is based on the notion that non-Christian peoples either have no conception of God, or do not believe in him. It is a generally pejorative term when applied to non-Christian peoples, suggesting that they are culturally, if not mentally, inferior, uncivilized, and benighted. In the 1930s and 40s it was an "in" word; and Barth may therefore be excused for using it. But those today working in the area of intercultural relations should generally avoid its use when referring to non-Western, non-Christian peoples.

Bibliography

Barth, Karl. *Church Dogmatics Volume IV: The Doctrine of Reconciliation, Part 3, Second Half.* G. W. Bromiley, trans. Edinburgh: T. & T. Clark Ltd., 1962.

_____. *Dogmatics in Outline.* G. T. Thompson, trans. New York: Harper & Row, 1959.

Costas, Orlando. *Theology of the Crossroads in Contemporary Latin America: Missiology in Mainline Protestantism: 1969-1974.* Amsterdam: Rodopi, 1976.

Part III
Focus on Ministry

The Christian Teacher
in the Church and World
T. Franklin Miller

Jesus was called Teacher more often than he was called anything else. He is our example. No one has more completely modeled the role of Christian teacher. To be asked to be a teacher is to be called to a high vocation. Rigorous and demanding, Christian teaching is also rewarding and delightful.

No other vocation counts so many in its ranks as does teaching. All parents are teachers, whether they know it or not. In many different settings teachers are at work with persons of all ages, from preschool children to older adults. Some are excellent teachers, some do poorly, many are only mediocre, but all are teaching. Governments spend vast sums on teaching, often using a captive audience and autocratic procedures for sophisticated indoctrination. Public schools, private schools, colleges, universities, seminaries— all are concerned with teaching. Teaching is the chief concern of many churches—from those whose self-image is a giant cookie-cutter turning out all look-alike and think-alike persons, to those who seek freedom of Christian personal development. Teaching is big business today. Maybe it always has been.

Teaching is not mere indoctrination or skill development, though the effectiveness of these elements must not be minimized. Adolf Hitler demonstrated the awesome power of mass indoctrination; scores of contemporary illustrations could be cited. What frightens many thinking persons is that the proven capability to "program" masses of people may be concentrated in and controlled by morally and ethically irresponsible leaders. Has that not already happened? Communicating ideas is already big business, but now we see millions who think, feel, and act like so many puppets controlled by a few stellar personalities. This prostituting of communication to mass production of paper-doll people gets us all to wear the same kind of jeans, sweaters, and tennis shoes, drink the same beverages, vote alike, and think like everyone else. But this is not teaching in the finest sense!

Geometric increase of knowledge staggers the mind, but it is not teaching. Storage, retrieval, reproduction, dissemination of that information by sophisticated and unimaginably swift means is not teaching. For millions uncounted, the teaching-learning experience has given way to cleverly manipulated propaganda. Dr. William Ernest Hocking, noted teacher and philosopher of Harvard, cited the development of propaganda as one of the four world-changing effects of World War I. How right he was! We witness and are victims of controlled propaganda in life-styles, religion, morality, relationships, family life, and the most intimate concerns.

Where is the Christian teacher? Is the Christian teacher as outdated as last night's news commentary? Is there any place for this once highly honored profession? Is it still a viable occupational choice? Does it have any lasting influence in this milieu of visual and audio bombardment?

The Christian Teacher

I

No one has taught until someone has learned, yet how many so-called teachers are simply pouring from the big jug into the little mugs. How many are concerned only that their students accept standardized religious ideas and behavior, quoting neat mathematical formulas and proof-text scriptures for every situation, all properly filed and indexed. Has such a one really taught? Has anyone really learned?

Dr. Carl Kardatzke, beloved professor at Anderson College and master teacher in the church school, reminded his students that Christian teaching must produce Christian ideas, attitudes, and actions. There is a gospel to communicate, a story to tell, a faith to share. The open mind is good, but as G. K. Chesterton said, "The point of an open mouth is to close it on something—and so with the open mind." Jesus applied this pragmatic test to teaching.[1]

This resultant cognitive, affective, and behavioral change Donald E. Miller said is the "new self replacing the old self," and "occurs only when a new set of values and beliefs has reorganized the persons' perception of himself and his world."[2] James Blair Miller pointed out that real learning will result in such changes as acquiring new knowledge or understanding, skill development, attitudes, interpersonal relationships, and behavior.[3]

The rapidity and magnitude of change are so great today that, as Paul Lengsand said, "change is now not only perceived by everyone in its practical implications, but is regarded as one of the basic experiences of the majority of human beings."[4] It subjects the teaching profession to constant fluctuations. Floods of new theories of learning and techniques constantly parade in enticing allure. What teacher cannot examine them, and like a fisherman before a tray of lures, wonder which of the new should be tried next.

Courage to experiment should be applauded, but it can be carried too far. In an earlier day interurban cars formed a network of rapid-rail transportation in some of the midwestern states. At night these cars roared through the countryside with powerful headlights tearing the curtains of darkness. One farmer had to move his chickens because they thought it was daybreak, and roosters were crowing at three o'clock in the morning. Others besides roosters have often crowed enthusiastically about false dawns.

A teacher needs to keep growing, which is far different from tasting samples, and growth will probably embrace changes in procedures. Charles Silberman thus calls for

> developing teachers' ability and their desire to think seriously, deeply, and continuously about the purpose and consequences of what they do—about the ways in which their curriculum and teaching methods, classroom and school organization, testing, and grading procedures, affect purpose and are affected by it. . . . Unless a teacher is also a student of teaching, he cannot grow as a teacher, an inspirer and director of soul life. . . . It is unreasonable, of course, to expect every educationist to be an inspiring teacher, let alone an inspiring human being; inspiration will always be in short supply. It is not unreasonable, however, to expect education faculties to take their job seriously—to expect them to think about educational purpose, and to arrange a curriculum that reflects their thought.[5]

We recognize the twin dangers of enslavement to innovation and to the accustomed; the former induces instability and frustration, the latter stagnation. It is the latter danger that Silberman emphasizes:

> Unless prospective teachers are given alternative pictures of what teaching and learning can be, along with the techniques they need to implement them, they are almost bound to teach in the same way their teachers taught them[6]

To say that we teach as we were taught, not as we were taught to teach, is to underline the impact of one personality upon another. Donald Rogers called for teachers to be in "constant refinement" of their work, of understanding the development of persons, and of using creative approaches. Then he continues:

The Christian Teacher

> But all of this follows and is in addition to the simple straightforwardness of being oneself. No technique is meant to replace persons and their natural and ordinary relationships. . . . In our mobile society, one loss we suffer is that of not being close enough to tell people how important they were to us (when we come to this realization down the pike). You, dear teacher, are going to be remembered in a humbling, appreciative way. You will be remembered for being there, for caring, for being yourself, and for teaching.[7]

Sometimes one who has grown up in a climate or religious authoritarian teaching will turn just the other way. One emerges from this suffocating environment in which all have to hold the same beliefs, act and think the same way, and, on breathing the fresh freedom, rebels against totalitarian disciplines. This teacher flounts a newfound liberation and sophistication in disdain for others. How many in the early days of high school or college have felt the sting of ridicule from such a teacher because their faith seemed simple and naive? Alexander Miller spoke of a faculty man who was either

> reared in a piety so authoritarian and constricting (fundamentalism) that he had to renounce it for the sake of his own intellectual freedom and integrity, or in a religious liberalism (modernism) so accomodated to the intellectual spirit of the times that he became a humanist almost without noticing the transition.[8]

One who has struggled through doubt and the highly regimented system of many churches and some schools ought, rather, to be patient with other pilgrims. It helps to remember that no cup can ever be filled unless it is filled gently.

One cannot stress too much the centrality of the teacher-pupil relationship in all teaching. We recall the words of President Garfield, "Give me a log hut, with only a simple bench, Mark Hopkins on one end and I on the other, and you may have all the buildings, apparatus, and libraries without him."[9]

We may forget what we were taught; we do not forget our teachers. This lays a double challenge on the teacher: to excel in teaching and to be a person worthy of imitation. In the early part of this century George Herbert Betts sounded this same call for teachers to attend to their character. He referred to the mind and spirit of the teacher as the "stained glass through which the sunlight must fall; all that passes through the medium of a living personality takes its tone and quality from this contact."[10]

This identification and interaction of teacher and student calls to mind a story Paul Rees told of a priest who served in a leper colony. For months he had no success in ministry. One day he contracted leprosy himself and word spread quickly. The chapel was then filled with lepers and conversions began to occur.[11] The importance of one's personal influence in teaching cannot be overstated. Dr. Elton Trueblood, himself a highly honored teacher, in speaking of this relationship said the greatest gift one "can provide others consists in being a radiant and encouraging person. What we are is more significant, in the long run, than what we do. It is impossible for a man to give what he does not have."[12]

Good teaching, then, begins with a good teacher, and the first mark of a good teacher is being a good person. Jesus, our best teacher, first exposed his disciples to the dynamics of his own life; his spirit, then, as now, was contagious. He chose twelve "that they might be with him."[13] He is still the teacher's model and tour guide on this adventure. We can share with others only that which was in turn shared with us by Christ: "forgiveness, hope, esteem, security, love, possessions, and the possibility of creative self-realization."[14]

Both teacher and student are learners, and they often learn from each other. The task of the teacher is not to indoctrinate the student, but to bear witness to faith in such a manner that reflection and further study are encouraged.[15] A high school physics teacher spoke so reverently about the laws of the universe thay many of his students were drawn to the Creator who was real to him. A fourth grade teacher's love for students was so redemptive it transcended faults and failures and left with some a lasting impression that her life was captured by a higher love. An eighth-grade music teacher not only encouraged an appreciation for great music, but inspired many students to seek her out privately for conversations about faith in God. A junior high teacher of English literature in reference to the development of the English Bible quietly carried her own witness of it as lamp to her feet and light to her path.

It may be objected that secular education allows no room for teaching values. Nonsense! Teachers and students are always involved in the valuing process. In selecting a text book or reference work, in developing a lesson plan, in choosing a teaching method the valuing process is always going on whether we like it or not. "Learning itself is a valuing process.[16]

Without so much as a hint that public schools or secular colleges should be used surreptitiously for sectarian teaching, we hold strongly the conviction that a Christian teacher, like Ruskin's view of a lamplighter, leaves a trail of light behind. Bushel baskets are made to measure apples and potatoes, not to obscure the light of faith. In every situation the Christian teacher will seek ways to give a witness to faith, even though it is never verbally articulated in the classroom. When one is Christian, one's life *is* teaching something about the Christian gospel.

A neighbor of David Hume once invited him to church to hear a former pastor, now retired. Later Hume was asked for his reaction. He replied that he had little use for religious worship, then added, "When that old man stood up to preach, he acted like he believed Jesus Christ was standing at his elbow." Any Christian teacher in any classroom anywhere could do that.

II

Earlier a reference was made to the rigorous demands of teaching that excels. It is hard work. Someone aptly said, "You cannot fly like an eagle with the wings of a wren." It *is* work—hard work—to achieve intellectual integrity and emotional maturity; it is work to master effective methods of communication. It is work to enter with empathy into the needs of a student; it is work to keep abreast of the ever-changing and new. It is not easy to be a real Christian in any classroom today. Who ever said it would be easy? What Halford Luccock said of a preacher is equally true of the Christian teacher: "One of the priceless equipments of a preacher is a limp of the sort that Jacob got from wrestling with an angel. Toiling at a craft with intensity is wrestling with the angel of the Lord."[17]

Van Wyck Brooks, speaking of the same effort to master his craft, said, "Every day I begin my work with the same old feeling, that I am on trial for my life and will probably not be acquitted."[18]

To achieve and maintain creativity in Christian teaching is painfully hard. As Balzac said, it is to "toil like a miner under a landslide," but it is most rewarding. A scripture in Jeremiah as applied to the Christian teacher has a dismal note of gloom for those who look for the easy way: "Cursed be the one who does the Lord's work negligently."[19]

Jesus had little patience with slipshod work and certainly did not expect his disciples to be "shiftless, make-it-do people," as he ridiculed putting a patch on an old garment and building a house without proper foundations, and told his story of the silly people with half-filled lamps.[20] He spoke of a narrow gate and disciplined living. People were amazed at his teaching; so may they be again of a disciplined teacher. The call has not changed.[21] Resources for improving in teaching are uncountable; how little they are used. Is the parable of the talents relevant here? The severest condemnation was given to the one who failed to develop what he was given.[22]

Elton Trueblood, speaking of Albert Schweitzer as a teacher, said, "Always the advice is that of refusing to settle for littleness when magnitude is possible."[23] This is a far cry from the casual approach of teachers who are like Mr. Micawber in Dickens's *David Copperfield*, who wanted to "be ready in case anything turns up."[24] What does this say to us about preoccupation with job benefits? What does it say of the temptation to "coast on in" once tenure is obtained?

Whether in a classroom in kindergarten, college, or seminary, whether the subject is reading, trigonometry, philosophy, or music, the disciplined Christian teacher takes the work seriously as a ministry. The setting may be a Sunday school class, a Christian college, high school, or state university——the Christian teacher carries a witness and makes an impact *because of being a Christian teacher*. The witness of the Apostle Paul was as articulate and effective in a hostile courtroom as in a foul dungeon, on the slippery planks of a sinking ship as in the warm embrace of fellow Christians in worship. Harry Emerson Fosdick, writing of that great Christian teacher and philosopher Rufus Jones, said,

> He possessed the spiritual vitality he pled for, and he shared it. What he himself said, thinking of Phillips Brooks, was true of him—"you listen to a hundred persons unmoved and unchanged. You hear a few quiet words from the man with the kindling torch and you suddenly discover what life means, forever more, and you become forthwith another man—carrying perhaps your own torch."[25]

Is it too much to hope that for the Christian teacher the more difficult the situation and the more unpromising the student, the greater the challenge to succeed? Thousands of Christian teachers daily face the difficult, sick, undisciplined, and uncaring student. When all else in that student's life is pulling downhill, just a holding operation may be success! Any effort to counteract the negative forces in environment, past failures, or attitude will not be in vain.[26]

Look again at the parable of the talents.[27] Two servants were commended for developing what they were given and using that capital investment as careful stewards; the final reward perhaps came as a surprise to them. This ought to be an encouragement to a Christian teacher. It is like dropping a stone in a pool of water: the splash, the event, is soon gone but the waves forever change the pool. The word is spoken, the deed is done, but the influence lives on and on. So the Christian lives as a responsible steward, gives one's best to the job, and leaves the results with God. Not in this life will one see all of those results.

In 1891 when Senator and Mrs. Leland Stanford opened the university to which they gave their name, they cared deeply that religion would be included in the curriculum and that faculty members would be thoroughly Christian in character and in teaching methods. Speaking of it, Mrs. Stanford expressed a determination since echoed by many other administrators:

> A man with an education and without morals is liable to become—indeed, he is almost sure to become—simply an abler, shrewder criminal, whose ability to prey upon society has been increased by education.[28]

She went on to say how much that education should be influenced by people committed to the Christian faith, and that such an experiment in the fruitful relations of faith and learning might become "a breeding ground for men and women in whose hearts and minds these issues are real," and as these people "fan out through the whole territory of higher education they may well bring to it new illumination on the problems that so sorely vex it."[29] Well, the intervening years have unfolded quite a story, but have left us with the conviction that, tough as it is, Christian teaching—Sunday school, elementary public school, high school, college, seminary—is still some of society's saving salt. One who doubts its effectiveness might try removing the salt from a hamburger or bowl of soup.

Christian teaching is never easy, but it stands as one of the last best hopes of humankind.

III

Perhaps all communicators often feel they are just the channels through which ideas are mediated. Ruskin said of great artists, "Their power is not so much in them but through them." George Eliot said, "My predominant feeling is—not that I have achieved anything, but—that great, great facts have struggled to find a voice through me, and only been able to speak brokenly." Ralph Waldo Emerson confessed that he felt that a flowing river poured its streams into him, and that he was "not a cause, but a surprised spectator" of what was happening and put himself in the "attitude of reception, but from some alien energy the visions come."[30]

If this is true of writers, artists, musicians, teachers, how much more so for the Christian teacher.. In addition to feeling the struggle of ideas for adequate expression, one is aware of being an instrument for the ministry of the Holy Spirit. This awareness and a sense of the stewardship of time will keep a Christian teacher conscious of the danger of vacuity in presentation. When Thoreau was at Walden Pond in Massachusetts, his meditation was interrupted by the noise of workmen installing telegraph poles. He was told they were putting in a long-distance telegraph line from Maine to Texas. "But suppose," he said, "when it is completed the people of Texas have nothing to say to the people of Maine, and the people of Maine will have nothing to say to the people of Texas!" Ah, that is an ever-present danger, isn't it? Technology has given the tools for swift and effective communication; it cannot tell us *what* to say.

For the Christian teacher this urges dependence upon the Holy Spirit. Long ago our Lord shared his plan for meeting this deep need of all Christian teachers.[31] This does not excuse one from careful preparation; rather one is under greater responsibility just because of the ministry of the Holy Spirit.[32]

The Holy Spirit also gives adequacy. A small boy was trying to move a big table, and his father said, "You can't move that—it's as big as you are." The boy, undaunted, said as he pushed, "I can, too, I'm as big as the table." That does not change the size of the table, but it does influence one's ability to move it! This self-confidence is not from arrogance or pride, but the power of the Holy Spirit.

During World War II Dr. Samuel Shoemaker learned that one of his wealthy parishioners lost the cook to whom she had been accustomed. As the pastor greeted her he asked how the food preparation was doing, and she said all was going well. "It is amazing," she said, "how much the fire does." How many, especially teachers, have been amazed at what the Holy Fire does! They reaffirm daily the testimony of the Apostle Paul, "I can do all things through him who strengthens me."[33]

The role of the teacher, then, is to be the servant, the instrument, through whom the Holy Spirit works. The teacher is not the noble pontificator from whom the student will sponge up some learning.[34] One is not the fountainhead of all knowledge; that idea is gone with the knowledge explosion, rapidity of change, the efficiency of machines and technological improvements, and the great increase in what students know before they ever start to school. The role is thus that of guide, coach, helper, aide, assistant in the teaching-learning situation. The teacher is an enabler, a door-opener.[35] Nothing will delight such a teacher more than to kindle the torch and see one's students surpass all the achievements of the teacher. The joy of this person is like that of John the Baptist in recognizing that Jesus had to increase while he decreased.[36] Like Moses on Mount Nebo he knows that the promised land he views will be possessed by others whom he has led thus far. And he will rejoice in their victories.

The Christian Teacher

The Holy Spirit kindles one's imagination regarding the possibilities in persons. Consider how Jesus took those who appeared to be ordinary, untalented, not gifted, called them, coached, and challenged them. The Christian teacher is thus in great company.

The indicators in a student's profile may be so limiting as to discourage most teachers from investment of energy. Dr. Robert H. Reardon, honored president emeritus of Anderson College and himself a superior teacher, once in speaking to a group of Christian teachers urged them to seek out and develop these hidden possibilitites. He said, "Your job is to prove the indicators are wrong." This is the nudging of the Holy Spirit. As encourager God stands beside us in this difficult but rewarding effort to discover and develop latent possibilities. Some of us have heard in Africa an ancient proverb that any fool can count the apples on a tree, but only the wise can count the trees in an apple. The Holy Spirit helps the teacher count trees.

IV

Some of us are tempted to live and teach like hermits in isolation from the world. That is like the recruiting advertisements Dr. Reardon used to tell about in referring to a college that said they were located twenty miles from any known form of sin! Some leaders, appalled with the evils of society and the secularization of public education, have retreated into their own school systems. This does provide a sheltered environment for a few years, but eventually all of us do move into the mainstream of life, into a world with sin and evil.

Our purpose in Christian teaching is to equip persons for living in and coping with the world as redemptive agents of change. Jesus reinforced this role in his reference to salt, leaven, and light as powerful images of the Christian's redemptive witness.[37] While some retreat with John the

Baptist to the seclusion of the wilderness, Christian teachers are really called to walk with Jesus into the world's market places to bear witness. Alvin Toffler was speaking of how to meet change and prepare for the future, but he might have been speaking of these special concerns of ours:

> The ultimate purpose of futurism in education is not to create elegantly complex, well ordered, accurate images of the future, but to help learners cope with real-life crises, opportunities, and perils. It is to strengthen the individual's practical ability to anticipate and adapt to change, whether through invention, informal acquiescence, or through intelligent response.[38]

This awareness of the needs of society and of the imperatives of the Christian gospel is fundamental to our work. This is, in part, the burden of Dr. Reuel Howe's call for use of the principle of dialogical teaching. He asks for continued dialogue between teacher and student, but chiefly in the context of that student's needs in contemporary society.

> To read contemporary news and comment thoughtfully and not read the Bible meditatively is to be irresponsible as a citizen; and to read the Bible meditatively and not read the news and comment responsibily is to read the Bible irresponsibly. The Bible was born out of the meeting of the news of the day and word of God. Likewise the participation in contemporary life needs the illumination of the Bible just as the understandings of the Bible call for participation in the making of contemporary history.[39]

This emphasis is being called for in many places, such as Howard Grimes as he speaks of the conversations needed between educators and theologians,[40] and Jesse Ziegler in his concerns for adequate adult education.[41] Indeed, contemporary leaders in Christian teaching are now saying that this crossing point of the gospel and the human situation is the moment of learning and growing.

Some Christian leaders went to the top of Pike's Peak with a friend who lived in a town at the base of the mountain. Caught up in the grandeur and majestic beauty of the Colorado Rockies, their meditative mood was shattered by the cry of their friend who had spotted his house far below. "Hey, look, that's where I live," he cried out. One of the others said he felt like saying "Who cares where you live—I was in worship." Another, in reflective perception, said that must always happen. Great teaching is when the gospel and human need intersect and somebody exclaims, "Hey, look, that's where *I* live!"

In the struggling interaction of the gospel and the human situation, learning and growth occur in the Christian life. The New Testament, thoroughly conversant with the tragedy and hurt of lost and bewildered people, is even more at home with its message of redemption. Visitors to Rome usually see the Sacra Scala, the church of the sacred stairs, which are supposed to be the ones Jesus climbed to Pilate's judgment hall. Constantine had them brought to Rome and made the central part of a church building. Searching pilgrims come to climb the stairs on their knees, saying a prayer on each stair. At the top is the altar. The pilgrim hopes to find forgiveness and peace at the end of the painful ascent. John R. Mott, world Christian lay leader, said that all ethnic religions call for the upward struggle to peace and wholeness. The Christian gospel, he said, starts with God at the top, coming down the long altar stairs to where we live in sin, to offer redemption.

The Christian teacher is humbled by this supreme revelation and the Bible as the record of that revelation. There we stand beneath the cross—its horizontal beam reaching to the worst of all sinners—but take hope in the vertical, God's invasion of this rebellious race. The cross thus becomes a powerful symbol of the teaching ministry, the crossing point of Christ and the world, the intersection so earnestly sought as a moment of learning. Humankind's slow progress is a history of that witness at every such dangerous intersection. Seneca said, "A great pilot can sail even when his canvas is rent."[42] So the Holy Spirit takes our fumbling but honest attempts at guiding persons in their Christian growth, and again and again the bread and fish are miraculously multiplied to meet human need.

Every Christian teacher has aspirations for the students, goals for the ultimate development of their resident possibilities. What does the profile of the mature student look like? This is no plea for regimented learning, transmissive teaching, or assembly-line products, nor for reproduction of a model unless it be Jesus Christ himself. Are there, however, reasonable expectations? Here are some with which to start. No one will fulfill all, but perhaps they persist as goals.[43] One should:

1. Be a growing person.

2. Have confidence from a proper self-image; not arrogance or fawning self-deprecation, but awareness of who one is, what one can do, of vast resources to be appropriated for holy and creative living.

3. Have a value system consonant with the teachings of Jesus.

4. Have a world view respecting all persons, rising above parochial interests, climbing the ladder of relationship from acquaintance, knowledge and understanding, to empathy, appreciation, cooperation in common causes.

5. Hold the conviction that the Christian gospel is the hope of all humankind, not diminished in intensity by profound respect for all other religious beliefs.

6. See that Jesus Christ is our eternal contemporary; free from all sectarian smothering, he is relevant to all people everywhere.

7. Be aware that self-determination, fulfillment of personhood, peaceful pursuit of worthy aims, equitable access to food, clothing, housing, meaningful occupation, dignity, and democracy's basic freedoms are the birthright of everyone.

8. Hold a conviction that world peace can be guaranteed only by the sanctions of goodwill, understanding, and redemptive love.

9. Be involved in responsible citizenship.

10. See Christian stewardship of all resources as a life-style.

11. Hold a commitment to use knowledge and techno-logical developments for the highest good of all persons.

12. Where options may be exercised in vocational pur-suits, place service above self with a sense of mission, believing that God cares how life is invested.

13. Participate in a congregation of worshipers for nur-ture, fellowship, worship, study, witness, service.

14. Develop an appreciation for beauty.

15. Hold a transparent goodness, open to truth.

16. Nurture patience born of faith in the educative process.

With even some of these goals realized, one will feel that the investment of energy has paid generous dividends.

Kenneth E. Eble closes a well-written chapter on prepara-tion for teaching with a story the noted pianist Claudio Arrau tells about his early education.

> "The first two teachers in Berlin were boring," he told an interviewer. "I wanted only to read more music, to perform more music. At eight, I loved the piano so, I would take my meals at the keyboard. By ten, dull teaching had turned me against music and myself."
>
> "But you were rescued," the interviewer said.
>
> "Desperate at ten," Arrau continued, "I was taken to play for Martin Krause. He was a severe old man, but children feel reality, and behind this harsh mask was an incredible gift for opening up worlds."
>
> Few teachers can have pupils like Arrau, but all teachers can have the opportunity for opening up worlds.[44]

More than four decades since, someone handed me a clipping from what appeared to be a magazine of an educa-tion association, with name, date, and page missing. It was a prayer written anonymously by someone who was a teacher somewhere in a public school system. It has since been shared with many teachers in many settings in many countries; it is given again as a prayer for anyone who would be a Christian teacher in the Church and the world:

A Teacher's Prayer

O God, who hast ever brought all life to its perfection by patient growth, grant me patience to guide my pupils to the best in life.

Teach me to use the compulsion of love and of interest; and save me from the weakness of coercion.

Make me one who is a vitalizer of life and not a merchant of facts.

Show me how to overcome the forces that destroy by harnessing the urges that lead to the life abundant.

Give me such a sense of value that I may distinguish the things that last from those that pass, and never confuse mountains with molehills.

Grant me insight to overlook the faults of exuberance because I can see with prophetic eye the possibilities of enthusiasm.

Save me, O Lord, from confusing that which is evil with that which is only immature.

May I learn the laws of human life so well that, saved from the folly of reward and punishment, I may help each pupil of mine to find a supreme devotion for which he will give his all. And may that devotion be in tune with Thy purpose for Thy world.

May I be so humble and keep so young that I may continue to grow and to learn while I teach.

Grant that I may strive not so much to be called a teacher as to be a teacher; not so much to speak of Thee, but to reveal Thee; not so much to talk about love and human service, but to be the spirit of these; not so much to speak of the ideals of Jesus, but in every act of my teaching to reveal His ideals.

The Christian Teacher

Save me from letting my work become commonplace by the ever present thought that, of all human endeavors, teaching is most like the work that Thou hast been doing through all the generations.

Amen.

Notes

1. See such passages as Matthew 5:17-20; 7:16-27; Luke 6:39-49; 9:57-62; 13:1-9, 36-43; John 13:12-17.

2. Donald E. Miller, "Psychological Foundations for Christian Education," in *An Introduction to Christian Education*, Marvin J. Taylor, ed. (Nashville; Abingdon Press, 1966), 54.

3. James Blair Miller, "Teaching Resources for Christian Learning," in *An Introduction to Christian Education,* 219.

4. Paul Lengsand, *An Introduction to Lifelong Education* (London: Croom Helm, 1975), 98.

5. Charles E. Silberman, *Crisis in the Classroom* (New York: Random House, 1970), 472-3.

6. Silberman, p. 473.

7. Donald B. Rogers, *In Praise of Learning* (Nashville: Abingdon Press, 1980), 29, 30.

8. Alexander Miller, *Faith and Learning* (New York: Association Press, 1960), 129-30.

9. From an address by President Garfield to Alumni of Williams College, December 28, 1871, quoted by Burke A. Hinsdale in *President Garfield and Education*, p. 43. Mark Hopkins was president of Williams College, 1836-1872.

10. George Herbert Betts, *How to Teach Religion, Principles and Methods* (New York: Abingdon Press, 1916), 15.

11. As told by Keith Miller in *The Becomers* (Waco, Tex.: Word Books, 1973), 52.

12. Elton Trueblood, *The New Man for Our Time* (New York: Harper and Row, 1970), 79.

13. Mark 3:14.

14. Keith Miller, *The Becomers*, p. 176.

15. Beverly Welton, "Teaching for Self-Direction," in *Basics for Teaching in the Church* (Anderson, Ind.: Warner Press, 1968), 86.

16. Arthur W. Combs, *Myths in Education* (Boston: Allyn and Bacon, 1979), 82, part of a longer discussion of the valuing process in education.

17. Halford Luccock, *In the Minister's Workshop* (New York: Abingdon-Cokesbury, 1944), 36.

18. Van Wyck Brooks, *Opinions of Oliver Allston* (New York: E. P. Dutton and Co., 1941), 30.

19. Jeremiah 48:10.

20. See Matthew 7:24-29, 9:16, 17; Luke 17:7, 8.

21. Matt. 6:22-24; 7:18, 19; 10:16-25.

22. Matt. 25:14-30.

23. Trueblood, p. 43.

24. Charles Dickens in *David Copperfield* chap. 12.

25. Harry Emerson Fosdick, *Rufus Jones Speaks to Our Time*, an anthology (New York: The Macmillan Co., 1961), 11.

26. Arthur W. Combs, *Myths in Education*, see p. 204.

27. Matt. 25:14-30.

28. Alexander Miller, *Faith and Learning*, p. 123.

29. Alexander Miller, p. 124.

30. Harry Emerson Fosdick, *On Being a Real Person* (New York: Harper and Brothers, 1943), 214.

31. Arlo F. Newell, *Receive the Holy Spirit* (Anderson, Ind.: Warner Press, 1978). See p. 49.

The Christian Teacher

32. See John 15:26, 16:7-14.

33. Phil. 4:13.

34. Robert A. Dow, *Learning through Encounter* (Valley Forge, Pa.: Judson Press, 1971), 138.

35. Combs, see pp. 185-87.

36. John 3:30.

37. Matt. 13: 31-33.

38. Alvin Toffler, *Learning for Tomorrow: The Role of the Future of Education* (New York: Random House, Inc., 1974), 3.

39. Reuel L. Howe, "The Dialogical Foundations for Christian Education," in *An Introduction to Christian Education*, Marvin J. Taylor, ed. (Nashville: Abingdon Press, 1966), 91. This may also be some of the meaning of Pope John XXIII in his call for *aggiornamento*, (opening the windows for fresh air), at the Vatican Council II.

40. Howard Grimes, "Theological Foundations for Christian Education," in *An Introduction to Christian Education*, p. 40.

41. Jesse H. Ziegler, *Focus on Adults* (Elgin, Ill.: The Brethren Press, 1965), see p. 87.

42. Seneca, *Epistles* 30, 3.

43. This grows out of reflection upon Matthew 5, 6, 7; Romans 12; 1 Corinthians 13; 1 Timothy 4:16; Philippians 3:7—4:8.

44. Kenneth Eugene Eble, *The Craft of Teaching* (San Francisco: Jossey-Boss Publishers, 1981), 171.

On Being a Preacher
James Earl Massey

I.

Being a preacher connects us with a considerable body of rituals that can sometimes obscure a right view of ourselves. To begin with, ours is an authorized action. We speak as ordained persons, endorsed by some church body to serve freely in our role. For another thing, as authorized and endorsed persons we carry considerable sign value not only in our work but even in our physical presence. The very title *reverend* projects that sign value: the very mention of the word usually makes eyes move to take in the person so addressed—and those who look and listen are interested in the preacher's dress, demeanor, and tone of presence. As for dress, the practice of some to use the clerical collar still has profound effects, as do the proverbial dark suit, white shirt, and subdued tie in other circles in which the preacher is expected to show the signs in public dress.

Englishman Russell Brian has written,

> When it is desirable that we should think of and feel towards, particular individuals or classes of individuals in a special way, society tends to give them distinctive clothes, or uni-

forms. The effects of a uniform are both subtle and profound. A judge is not merely an elderly lawyer wearing a bizarre head-dress and a kind of overcoat dating from the remote past. His strange costume, because it is different from the clothes anyone else wears today, symbolizes his exceptional social function and powers; hence all who deal with him are confronted with an embodiment of society. The judge in court is something different in fact and feeling from the same man encountered on a social occasion. His professional *persona* is socially valuable, and his perceptual equipment contributes materially to it. The same is true of the priest, the policeman, and the postman, each in his different way.[1]

Society associates various meanings with certain functions, but in the case of the preacher's work we are really dealing with more than societal perceptions and expectations. In any discussion of the preacher's work we are dealing as well with the background factor of a call from God and authority from God to do what is being done, so that the sign value of any preacher becomes a reminder about God and what is associated with the divine.

Given the fact of our sign value as preachers, and given our right to handle and interpret the sacred texts in our special book, *The Holy Bible*, which contains and presents the very Word of God,[2] preachers experience a kind of positional privilege. As persons called and sent by God to speak his Word, our preaching becomes part of a hearer's *rite of passage*, as it were, into salvation. As Romans 10:14 puts it, "But how are men to call upon him in whom they have not believed? And how are they to believe in him of whom they have never heard? And how are they to hear without a preacher?" Such a verse does suggest that preaching is part of a hearer's *rite of passage* into the experience of salvation. Given this sign value, positional privilege, and strategic service role, the preacher must be careful to view the given work with honor, on the one hand, and oneself with humility, on the other.

Yes, the preacher is part of a special process of happenings. It is the plan of God that this is so. God uses his preachers to establish and reinforce faith, share understandings, stir persons to action, and relate to them in specialized ministries. But we can do these services best only when we demonstrate a disciplined commitment to the God who called and sent us. We must serve God and the people with the whole self durably engaged with God. Jesus referred to this as living with "a single eye" (Matt. 6:22).

II

In being a preacher, nothing can substitute for a settled intention and a God-committed life. Called to deal directly with persons in moral and spiritual matters—which includes cultural and social implications—we must know *what* to do and then *do* it as committed believers. The whole issue here has to do with integrity of role and humility of spirit.

I speak here as I do because we all know that it is possible for us to do something, even something worthy and necessary, without due sincerity and "clean hands." J. L. Austin, writing about this in another connection, pictured two crooks doing cover jobs in order to fulfill a deeper and devious intention. One crook was cleaning windows, the other was cutting trees, both were there only because they were "casing the place."[3] But we preachers must both *do* what is right and *be* right as we do it. We should be credible, committed persons, servants who can be heard and trusted gladly.

Franz Kafka wrote about his vision of a large city at night in which just a few people are awake. He likened it to a military encampment in which everyone is asleep except a few guards on duty keeping watch. Kafka asked why the few are still awake when all the others in the city are asleep; then he answered, "Because someone must be watching, someone must be there."[4] That was God's plan in calling and sending the preacher; someone needs to be watching. Someone needs to have a necessary word. Someone must be trustworthy, serving with integrity and humility.

III

I have touched again and again upon the need for a right view of ourselves and a humility to match the greatness of our work. Sooner or later we must come to the understanding that behind all that is involved in our work and witness is the grace of God, that we are what we are because God "judged [us] faithful by appointing [us] to his service" (1 Tim. 1:12). God called us not because we are great but because he is gracious.

But humility becomes us also because of our human limitations, or what Harry C. Howard has called "the incompleteness that inheres in human nature."[5] Although we experience the greatness of the call, the presence of gifts graciously bestowed upon us for service, and some margin of "success" as we work with integrity, over it all falls the shadow of our own frailty and incompleteness. We who preach hold this treasured ministry in frail hands and dying hearts. Whatever transcendent power that is associated with us belongs to God, not to us.

Humility, then, becomes the preacher in several ways:

1. Humility becomes us because *our gifts are limited.* Not one of us has all the gifts to make our ministry perfect and entire, lacking nothing. We must ever see and understand ourselves as but part of a larger whole. The ministry must be understood in its variety because a comprehensiveness embraces all whom God has chosen. Paul stated it like this: "Now there are varieties of gifts, but the same Spirit; and there are varieties of service, but the same Lord; and there are varieties of working, but it is the same God who inspires them all in every one" (1 Cor. 12:4-6).

2. Humility becomes us because *our individual effectiveness is limited.* No one preacher can draw *everyone* by his or her handling of the gospel. A law of attraction and appeal makes one and all effective—but within a limited scope. As Proverbs 18:16 puts it, "A man's gift makes room

for him," but that space is by circumstance and comparison limited and restricted. The church alive speaks to a world alive, and this demands persons of differing stations and gifts, which in turn means differences of appeal and limitations of influence. Each of us will have to learn our points of prowess and our points of need.

Given our limitations, we preachers must learn to regard and not criticize one another. Alexander Gammie used to tell about how the much-admired Dr. Alexander Whyte fondly treated the themes of sin and grace—and judged every other preacher by how he treated them. Once, while Whyte and Ralph Connor were walking and talking, the name of Henry Drummond entered the conversation. Whyte stopped in the path and, with a twinkle in his eyes, said, "The trouble with Hen-a-ry is that he doesna ken onything about sin."[6] I will not judge the truth or falsity of the criticism; I only suggest that Whyte was criticizing Drummond against *his* measuring themes. Such criticizing is quite often a serious weakness, the result of a limited view of another preacher's ministry, and a lack of appreciation for his or her place in the ministry. Limited as we all are in gifts and effectiveness, we must learn to show more love and appreciation for one another.

3. Humility becomes us because *our presence and physical powers are limited*. Paul admitted his limitations in this area (if our usual reading of 2 Corinthians 10:10 is correct):[7] "For they say [he argued], 'His letters are weighty and strong, but his bodily presence is weak, and his speech of no account.' " In repeating this jibe from some of his opponents about himself, Paul has given us our only reliable New Testament evidence about his appearance. We therefore understand that some of his opponents were so crass that they plagued the Apostle with insults about his physical appearance, making a jibe of his epilepsy, eye disease, malarial infection, or disfigurement from having been stoned. But Paul had learned to live with his physical problems and do his work in spite of them.

191

Preachers have their physical benefits or problems, and the way we handle those gifts or problems will often influence the way people will view and regard or criticize us. Scotsman James Macgregor thought at first that his short, twisted, and deformed legs would consign him to some out-of-the-way place for ministering, fearing that his physical appearance would be reprehensible to parishioners. But he went on to fame as pastor for forty years at St. Cuthbert, a large and outstanding church.[8] Spiritual endowment can outrank physical limitations—if we let it. No handicap of body need hinder the holiness of the preacher's mission under God.

James Morison, of Glasgow fame, also learned this. After suffering an injury in his vocal chords, Morison's voice was thereafter low and coarse and generally weak, although at times while speaking, his larynx became heated and his voice seemed closer to the old sound.[9]. But although his tone was not as orchestrated as before, Morison remained encouraged and his language attractive and his content rich. He made sure that when his hearers had to strain to hear him it would be worth their effort and *his*. With what uneasiness are you wrestling as you think about your vocal equipment?

Or are you plagued by a debilitating nervousness? So was R. W. Dale (1829-1895), of Carr's Lane, Birmingham, fame. Dale had problems with his nerves before becoming pastor of Carr's Lane, but working under John Angell James as assistant was not the easiest ministry, and his times of depression and deep inward struggle increased. Dale's problem was rooted in his sensitive temperament. Later, in his old age, Dale advised his own assistant George Barber, "Give God thanks for your temperament."[10] He was advising out of his own sad experience of nervous collapse that happened when he took the pastorate on his own—just into his thirties. The experience mellowed Dale for a more caring ministry, but he had to watch himself with great care across the rest of his years.

On Being a Preacher

Frederick William Robertson (1816-1853) also suffered from a highly sensitive nervous system that caused him to be intensely inward and increasingly distant at times. Later in his life an abscess developed at the base of his brain, which made an already problematic life and ministry more so. In one of the last letters Robertson wrote before his early death, he gave his advice to a friend about the handling of physical problems:

> It is a wise man's duty to try to work within his limitations in the best way he can, and grumble as little as possible: or else cut himself asunder at once from all restrictions and obligations, by giving up his sphere of work entirely.[11]

We cannot overlook our physical limitations, if we have them, as we seek to fulfill our ministry; but grace for dealing with them is our portion as we seek it. Grace *must* cover our handling of our limitations because the way people regard or criticize our apparent physical troubles can affect our judgment of them—if not ourselves. Not every handicapping circumstance or bodily condition can be mastered, but we can master our feelings about the way other persons regard or criticize them.

4. Humility becomes the preacher because, despite our training and experience, *our knowledge is limited.* Like Paul, we are wise to admit that "our knowledge is imperfect" (1 Cor. 13:9), and that we now only know "in part" (13:12). However much we study and inquire, probing long and thinking deeply, we still know all too little after the most exhaustive research.

Whenever I think very long about the problem of our limited knowledge, I recall the life and work of Joseph Butler (1692-1752), author of *The Analogy of Religion.* Butler wrote the *Analogy* during England's time of Deistic scepticism, a time when theological individualism was being lived to the extreme. Disturbed about the flippant irreligion of his people, Butler set himself to grapple with the problem of relating reason and faith. In one chapter he wrote about the probability argument as it relates to the biblical doctrine of a future life. There he acknowledged that nature has locked us out from having a full or demonstrable knowledge of what lies beyond death; meanwhile he asserted that being alive *now* is reason for a strong probability that we shall continue to live.[12]

Some years later, facing death, Butler desired a heart-assurance to help him face the hereafter. He was fearful of that future, armed only with his argument about a logical probability that his life would continue. Alexander Whyte reported Butler's deathbed conversation: upon summoning his chaplain, the dying bishop confessed, "Though I have endeavored to avoid sin, and to please God to the utmost of my power; yet from my consciousness of perpetual infirmities, I am still afraid to die."

"My lord," said the chaplain, "you have forgotten that Jesus Christ is a Savior."

"True," Butler replied, "but how should I know that he is a Savior for me?"

The chaplain strongly declared, "My lord, it is written, Him that cometh to Me, I will in no wise cast out."

"True," the bishop answered, "and I am surprised that though I have read that Scripture a thousand times over, I never felt its virtue till this moment. And now I die happy."[13]

Logic had become secure in realized love, and probability had found its rest in assurance. This was the needed deep knowledge. This was the assurance to which the gospel gives birth. As John H. Jowett rightly explained,

> We need an experimental knowledge of God. There must be something solid and satisfying. *We must know something,* something about which we can be dogmatic, and about which we can speak in words and tones of assurance.[14]

Our knowledge is limited; we do know only "in part," but we do know that much. We will learn more as we stay with God and remain open to life and grace, thorough in our faith and faithfulness.

5. Carefulness and humility become us because *our time to live and serve is limited.* Our steps are marked and our days are numbered. Despite the greatness of our work—and preaching is indeed a service of high honor—and despite the faithfulness we apply to it all, the time must come when we will be forced by life to let it all go and die. Erik Erikson has called attention to the "ego-chill" we each experience in talking about or facing the fact of our own death.[15] It is no small matter to deal with death in the first-person, but we, too, must one day move beyond talking about death and actually die, using our faith to cope.

In one of his writings W. Robertson Nicoll mentioned the plea of a certain minister-author as he submitted the last sheets of a new manuscript to the publisher: "And now, I pray you, do your part of the work quickly, for ministers are soon forgotten."[16] The very truth of that can also cause a painful ego-chill. Yes, carefulness and humility should indeed mark out lives as we serve our Lord.

IV

It is no small matter to be a preacher, to be "approved by God to be entrusted with the gospel" (1 Thess. 2:4), to handle its meanings as official ambassadors. William Brewing has asked these questions:

> Who else deals with the whole man—body, mind, soul and spirit? Who else encompasses the whole universe, seen and unseen, in life's analysis? Who else measures life, not in scales of material, temporal values, but in terms of eternal treasures?[17]

What a trust indeed, and an undeserved privilege!

I thought deeply about this privilege and trust I have experienced through grace as I stood some years ago at the bedside of a thirty-eight-year-old mother dying from acute leukemia. It was an oppressively hot Detroit day, and since the hospital room was not air-conditioned the windows were all raised. The nurse attending my member had left the room when I entered, knowing my mission during her final moments of life.

For a while I was all-too conscious of the noisy after-work traffic speeding along on the bustling freeway just below the room, so I stood closer to the bed to hear and speak more readily. The young mother recognized me as I called her name. She stirred gently, returned a greeting with a weak voice, even managed a characteristic smile, and haltingly spoke about what she was experiencing at the moment. As I listened to her I knew that *she was trying to help me become witness to what was so evident to her in her dying hour.* She was in midpassage, moving inwardly between this earthly realm and life's next level, and she was trying to brief me on what she was hearing and seeing there.

It was a mystical moment, a moment of high drama! I knew that I did not need to be concerned about her emotional well-being. There was no denial of death, no bargaining, no anger, no depression, but an active acceptance of it all as an assured Christian believer.

I held her hand as her words ebbed and flowed in weak voice, and I finally quoted a string of great texts of strength from the Bible we both know and loved. And then, after a certain text of promised divine presence, I heard her say to me, "Yes, it is so . . . because he is here . . . with me . . . now. Do you see him, too?" she asked.

And I, hindered, blocked, forbidden by circumstance, had to answer, "No, my sister; but I understand what you are saying. I cannot see him because he has come for *you.* This is *your* moment! This is all for *you!* This is *your* time!"

Then silence fell—and something more! Even the traffic noise from the busy freeway below suddenly faded from my consciousness and *I found myself caught up into her moment of passage into eternity!* My whole being tingled as if charged by an electric current and I felt the pulse-beat of eternity within myself! I was in another realm and in tune with a higher order! It was a moment of experienced glory!

On Being a Preacher

When I "came to myself," as we say, I knew a level of tie with the next life that I had not known before. Having opened myself to the meaning of her home-going, I found myself lifted to new levels of awareness about the really important things in life *here* and the invitational pull of the eternal dimension *beyond.* That brief but unforgettable encounter with *that other side* of life gave me a deep appreciation for *this* side, and a deeper awareness of what being a preacher means to help people get ready for life in full.

That day in that hospital room made a world of difference in my diligence and devotion. That young mother died shortly after I left the room, and I continue to thank God for that grand hour of spiritual togetherness in his presence as her spirit was being lifted into that higher realm. Any preacher who has had similar experiences with Christians in their dying hours knows that death only chilled the body, not the soul. That preacher also senses more deeply the eternal importance of what we have been called and entrusted by God to be, say, and do.

> A charge to keep I have,
>   A God to glorify;
> A never-dying soul to save,
>   And fit it for the sky.
>
> To serve the present age,
>   My calling to fulfill—
> O may it all my pow'rs engage
>   To do my Master's will!
>
> Arm me with jealous care,
>   As in thy sight to live;
> And O thy servant, Lord, prepare,
>   A strict account to give!
>
> Help me to watch and pray,
>   And on thyself rely,
> Assured if I my trust betray
>   I shall forever die.[18]

Notes

1. *The Nature of Experience* (London: Oxford University Press, 1959), 46.

2. On the concept of Holy Book, see *Holy Book and Holy Tradition,* F. F. Bruce and E. G. Rupp, eds. (Grand Rapids: Wm. B. Eerdmans Publishing Co., 1968), esp. pp. 1-19.

3. See J. L. Austin, *Philosophical Papers* (Oxford: Clarendon Press, 1961), chap. 9. Bernard Mayo has discussed Austin's illustration in his "The Moral Agent" in *The Human Agent,* vol. 1 (New York: St. Martin's Press, 1968), esp. pp. 58-62.

4. Cited by Thomas E. Clarke, S.J., *New Pentecost or New Passion? The Direction of Religious Life Today* (New York and Toronto: Paulist Press, 1973), 58-59.

5. *Princes of the Christian Pulpit and Pastorate* (Nashville: Cokesbury Press, 1928), 238.

6. Alexander Gammie, *Preachers I Have Heard* (London: Pickering and Inglis, Ltd., n.d.), 12.

7. The grammatical difficulties in the Greek text do not allow for a final settlement of the question raised here of whether the diatribe word *phēsin* is a supposed objector of a real one. I have proceeded on the belief that the objector was real.

8. See Gammie, p. 25.

9. Gammie, p. 61.

10. See Harry D. Howard, p. 280.

11. Stopford A. Brooke, *Life and Letters of Frederick W. Robertson* (London: Kegan Paul, Trench, Truebner and Co., Ltd., 1891), vol. 2, p. 219. See also James R. Blackwood, *The Soul of Frederick W. Robertson: The Brighton Preacher* (New York: Harper, 1947). 167-80, which treats Robertson's death from the brain malady.

12. *The Works of Joseph Butler,* W. E. Gladstone, ed., vol. 1 (Oxford: Clarendon Press, 1896), p. 24. Chapter 1, pp. 19-47,

contains Butler's full statement about "Of a Future Life," which is discussed from the viewpoint of probability.

13. See Alexander Whyte, *With Mercy and with Judgment* (London: Hodder and Stoughton, n.d.), 269-70. See also Whyte's *Thirteen Appreciations* (Edinburgh and London: Oliphant, Anderson and Ferrier, n.d.), 278, 280.

14. *The Preacher: His Life and Work* (New York: Harper, 1912), 199. The italics are Jowett's.

15. See his *Young Man Luther* (New York: W. W. Norton and Co., Inc., 1958), 111.

16 *Princes of the Church* (London: Hodder and Stoughton, Ltd., 1921), 304.

17. "The Sermon I Might Have Preached, If!" in *Here Is My Method: The Art of Sermon Construction,* Donald Macleod, ed. (Westwood, N.J.: Fleming H. Revell Co., 1952), 37.

18. Charles Wesley, "A Charge to Keep I Have."

James Earl Massey

Continuing Education: A Hedge Against Boredom in Ministry

Jerry C. Grubbs

BOREDOM IN THE MINISTRY

This is an exciting time to be a minister of the gospel! No, that affirmation is not the naive beating of a lonely drummer. Many persons from a variety of places and styles are discovering the joy and satisfaction of Christian ministry.

For countless others, however, this is not the case. They wander aimlessly from day to day, doing what has become for them routine, dull, and boring.

We cannot ignore the turbulent state of ministry in today's world. In a real sense, there is an identity crisis among ordained clergy.[1] The local church pastor is no longer the parson or distinctive person in the community. No longer is the pastor the best-educated person in the congregation or community. Although often called *reverend,* the minister is seldom revered.

Scores of other helping professions have emerged in the community. What does the professional clergy have to offer as just one among many attempting to meet human needs?

Evidence suggests that some local parish ministers have forsaken their calling and the biblical role of pastor-teacher to become corporation executives. Granted, the corporation that they run is a local church. But they do so in the pattern of an organizational administrative *whip* rather than the biblical model of servant-leader.[2] They find their greatest excitement (thus, a hedge against boredom) in *avant garde* programming or a high-powered building program. When the excitement dies down, they settle back into a dull, boring routine until they can dream up another fascinating administrative ploy. Burned out and disillusioned by public-relations activities, meetings, and mimeograph machines, they die but go on pastoring.[3]

Conversations among clergy about relevance, renewal, revival, and reform are common. These conversations usually center around the latest how-to success story. Little mention is made of the biblical nature of the Church or the purpose of ministry. Where the church is or should be going is not clear.

Perhaps some clergy have lost the ability to think critically about ministry. One is reminded of a comment attributed to George Santayana that a fanatic is a person who has lost sight of his goal and redoubled his effort to get there. Such lack of purpose and meaning creates the devastating state of boredom in ministry.

A further tragedy is that many clergy do not know *why* they are bored. They only know that they *are* and continue merely reenacting with little enthusiasm, a script that is familiar and expected of them. From all appearances they are highly energetic, but idle; in motion, but going nowhere.

Clergy, like all humans, need to be aware that boredom is not really traceable to external forces such as lack of opportunity, poor facilities, small groups, low budgets, and the like. Rather, boredom is more accurately traceable to a lack of personally developed imagination and purpose. That is, boredom is an internal problem and not an environmental one.

Continuing Education

There *is* a hedge against boredom in ministry. Through the continuing and intentional development of one's own imagination, one's own resources as a person, one's own goals and purposes, and one's own aspirations, the once pointless passage of time can be turned into creative time. The alternative is to settle for haphazard episodes of excitement, entertainment, or gratification interrupted by long periods of dreary, dull, repetitive routine.

One significant key to avoiding boredom in ministry is continuing education. It is a key available to all who would claim it.

WHAT IS CONTINUING EDUCATION?

John is faithful in attending the regional meetings of clergy in his denomination. Guest speakers are recruited each year with some particular theme to be considered. The fellowship is rich and he regularly returns home with new ideas for preaching and programming.

Bonnie seldom misses an opportunity to attend the training seminars sponsored by her denominational board of education. She is convinced of the need to discover new and better ways to teach and administer educational ministries in the local church.

Ron was talking to a ministerial colleague at a recent meeting. The colleague suggested a book that had been especially helpful to him. Ron purchased the book and read it.

Rita graduated from seminary a few years ago. She is presently auditing a class in New Testament at a local seminary.

Robert is enrolled for one unit of CPE (Clinical Pastoral Education) through a local hospital. He is developing counseling skills under careful supervision.

Which of the previously mentioned activities is *continuing education?* The answer, of course, is that each one is continuing education. On the one hand, experiences like these and a myriad of others can rightly be considered continuing education. On the other hand, continuing education is more than a random selection and involvement in activities. It is important to understand continuing education a bit more clearly.

Mark Rouch has developed a helpful definition.

> Continuing education is an individual's personally designed learning program which begins when basic formal education ends and continues throughout a career and beyond. An unfolding process, it links together personal study and reflection and participation in organized group events.[4]

Rouch's definition contains a number of key phrases. An exegesis of several of these will further clarify the definition.

Continuing education is *personal.* That is, the responsibility for continuing education rests primarily with the individual and not with some outside force or agency. Motivation for growth in ministry must come from within the person. Seldom are denominational mandates effective in bringing about significant involvement in continuing education.[5] The design for continuing education is not independent of the individual. Rather, after careful personal assessment, each person chooses those experiences that would best meet the needs identified in the assessment process.

Learning is a fundamental ingredient in continuing education. Random experiences involving little or no reflection are not considered continuing education. Intentional and planned experiences calling for critical thinking, effective choices, and responsible action best describe continuing education.

In its technical understanding, continuing education in the professions *begins whenever the basic formal education ends.* So, continuing education for physicians would begin upon graduation from medical school and establishment of medical practice, for lawyers upon graduation from law school and establishment of a law practice, for nurses upon receiving a basic nursing degree, and so on. However, since entry requirements into professional ministry are diverse and not so clearly defined, it is more difficult to pinpoint the beginning of continuing education for ministry. Nevertheless, once a person has embarked upon professional ministry as a vocation, all intentional learning experiences are within the definition of continuing education.

Continuing education for ministry is *a life-long process.* The need for personal growth in ministry does not end. Margaret Mead has written, "No one will live all his life in the world into which he was born, and no one will die in the world in which he worked in his maturity. . . . In today's world, no one can complete an education."[6] Those of us in theological education are quite aware that about half of what we teach theological students will become obsolete in ten years. The problem is that we do not know which half. One solution to this dilemma is to guide students in the development of personal skills that will enable them to be life-long self-directed learners.

One may choose to develop one's continuing education around *personal study and reflection or participation in organized groups.* A variety of combinations of methodologies can be used. More will be said on this subject later.

In order for continuing education as previously defined to be effective, two distinct changes must occur in traditional educational *modus operandi.* First, persons must be ready, willing, and capable of assuming responsibility for their own learning. And second, persons must break out of the stereotyped notion that effective learning requires the structure of a classroom setting.

THE CONTENT OF CONTINUING EDUCATION

The statement was made earlier that continuing education is personal. Thus, the content of continuing education emerges out of the persons involved in ministry. Who is the minister?[7]

Ministers are often discussed according to the various roles they fulfill. Thus, one might speak of the minister as preacher, pastor, priest, and politician. The Episcopal church talks about the minister's roles as preacher, priest, leader of worship, equipper, interpreter, counselor, pastor, and celebrator.[8]

Others are more specific and choose to refer to the minister as "the wounded healer"[9] or "the pastor-theologian."[10] Educators often refer to the minister as "the key-educator."

The following descriptors have been chosen in an attempt to focus more on the *person* of the minister and less on the roles of the minister. Admittedly, this is a difficult task. After each descriptor are competencies that are needed to *be* the person described. Development of these competencies becomes the agenda for continuing education in ministry.[11]

1. *The Minister as Christian.* This involves a personal choice to follow Christ, to accept the clergy call, and to express one's values in life-style.

   Competencies Needed:
   (a) Development of an integrated theology;
   (b) Understanding of call to ministry:
   (c) Ability to choose and act upon values;
   (d) Openess to spiritual growth and renewal;
   (e) Skills in personal prayer and meditation.

2. *The Minister as Responsible Person.* This implies authenticity, personal integrity, and responsibility. Other personal traits include flexibility and humility, and a positive hopefulness about life and ministry.

   Competencies Needed:
   (a) Self-awareness;
   (b) Understanding of human development;
   (c) Ability to deal with the tragic, painful, absurd, and meaningless dimension of life;
   (d) Skills in human relationships;
   (e) Ability to set personal and professional goals.

Continuing Education

3. *The Minister as Theologian.* This person is an open, dialogical, reflective, and critical thinker.

> *Competencies Needed:*
> (a) Skills needed to do critical thinking—knowing how to think;
> (b) Ability to employ effective interpretive methods to the literature of the Christian tradition;
> (c) Understanding of the historical and cultural context of Scripture and the Church through the centuries;
> (d) Understanding of the major theological and ethical questions of the Christian tradition;
> (e) Ability to apply scriptural resources in the quest for answers to major theological and ethical questions;
> (f) Skills in research of major problems, knowing where information is, how to access it, and how to deal with the mass of data coming from all directions;
> (g) Ability to read structurally and analytically;
> (h) Ability to communicate ideas clearly and concisely.

4. *The Minister as Pastor.* A pastor is a person who "feeds" (from the Latin, *pascera*) the people; that is, one who nurtures others toward personal wholeness.

> *Competencies Needed:*
> (a) Ability to identify symptoms of human hurt;
> (b) Sensitivity to identify with hurting persons and to stand with them in their need;
> (c) Ability to integrate knowledge from the social sciences with that of theology;
> (d) Skills in intervention and referral when faced with persons experiencing crisis.

5. *The Minister as Preacher-Teacher.* The preacher-teacher communicates the message of the gospel in ways that

enable persons to discover meaning in their life situations.

Competencies Needed:
(a) Skills in sermon preparation and delivery;
(b) Knowledge of communication processes and their application to religious communication;
(c) Ability to speak and write clearly and articulately;
(d) Understanding and effective use of a variety of media;
(e) Knowledge of how persons learn at various developmental levels;
(f) Understanding of basic curriculum-development principles;
(g) Ability to develop and utilize teaching plans.

6. *The Minister as Priest.* The priest calls the body of Christ to preparation and involvement in worship. Worship is the central, unifying experience of God's gathered people.

Competencies Needed:
(a) Understanding of the liturgical heritage of one's church;
(b) Knowledge of theological principles that provide the foundation for Christian worship;
(c) Skills in planning and leading public worship;
(d) Knowledge and ability to employ music with theological and aesthetic integrity;
(e) Ability to plan and incorporate into the church's worship life such events as birth, baby consecration, baptism, marriage, death, and the like.

7. *The Minister as Enabler.* The enabler facilitates the identification and development of gifts, skills, and competencies of persons in the congregation and administers the organizational tasks so as to involve all persons in the ministry of the congregation.

Continuing Education

Competencies Needed:
(a) Understanding of biblical principles for church organization and administration;
(b) Understanding of ways to facilitate shared leadership and decision making;
(c) Ability to organize planning processes including determining priorities, setting goals, and developing resources;
(d) Skills in recruitment, training, and placement of staff;
(e) Ability to manage conflict in ways that maximize the possibilities for constructive growth in conflict situations;
(f) Understanding of denominational structures and their relationship to local church ministry.

8. *The Minister as World Citizen.* The world citizen is aware that life is much too large to be parochial. His or her life is an authentic witness to the universal character of the Christian faith.

Competencies Needed:
(a) An understanding of the global character of the Christian faith;
(b) Awareness of the role of political power as a form of Christian presence;
(c) Sensitivity to the transcultural nature of the Christian faith;
(d) Understanding and appreciation of pluralism and skills in relating to persons and groups who express many diverse and often contradictory viewpoints and actions;
(e) Knowledge of the world economy and its systemic nature including the production and distribution of food, energy, natural resources, and the like;
(f) Knowledge of and skills in relating to various national and international issues, movements,

and systems, including the role of U. S. power in the affairs of the world.

It is important to note that the intended emphasis of this listing is on the person and not the role. Thus, an overarching goal in ministerial continuing education is that persons *become* before they seek to act out a particular role. Here is a listing of the eight descriptors:

1. The minister as Christian

2. The minister as responsible person

3. The minister as theologian

4. The minister as pastor

5. The minister as preacher-teacher

6. The minister as priest

7. The minister as enabler

8. The minister as world citizen.

Certainly this list is not all-inclusive or exhaustive. Other descriptors could have been chosen. The intent of the list is to give a starting point for considering the issue of the minister as a person.

Also, the forty-six competencies clustered under the eight descriptors are not complete. Others could be added, a few might be deleted, or some might need editing to be a bit more precise in their intent. Nonetheless, both the descriptors and competencies can serve as a valid starting point for thinking about and planning one's continuing-education program.

Personal assessment is a very important component of continuing education. It is not sufficient to hear the *shoulds* from other people. Other persons might be quite helpful to us in the process, but when the minister takes personal assessment seriously and does it thoroughly, he or she will discover the areas of needed growth. Then, due primarily to that inner motivation for competency, the minister is drawn to make effective choices about a continuing-education program.

Personal assessment needs to be a regular and on-going process. Changing values, places of ministry, developmental levels, and career stages all point to the need for the ongoingness of personal assessment.

The concept of career stages can be used to illustrate the need for ongoing assessment. Much more research is needed in regard to career stages as they relate to ministers. Therefore, the following diagram is not intended to reflect scientifically verified data. Rather, it illustrates how ministry might change as the minister goes through career stages.[12]

CAREER STAGES IN MINISTRY

STAGE	I	II	III	IV	V
AGE	18-25	26-40	41-55	56-65	65-
Description	Period of formal preparation	On trial by peers—getting settled and established in ministry. High energy	Midcareer period of productivity and advancement. Also some burn-out or changing vocations	Preretirement. Some retrenchment	Retirement changing status

Now, obviously, not all ministers enter Stage I precisely at age eighteen and exit at age twenty-five. However, this is a somewhat typical and illustrative process for a person whose career is ministry. The ages quite possibly could be pushed forward by late entry into a ministerial career. The assumption remains, however, that the career stages are still valid, although the ages might be compressed somewhat.

The point of all this is to suggest that as one assesses one's ministry within a given career stage, one will identify differing interests, needs, and motivations for involvement in continuing education. An assessment made in Stage I or

Stage II is not sufficient for planning a continuing-education program if one is presently in Stage IV.

Given the definition of continuing education and assumptions about the content of continuing education, how does the minister go about planning for continuing education? This is a question of major importance.

HOW DOES ONE PLAN FOR CONTINUING EDUCATON?

Some years ago, Connolly C. Gamble, Jr. observed that continuing education "involves a system or program. It must have a plan. It does not just happen—it requires deliberate conception. It seeks for an order that will make study consecutive and cumulative. It adopts a purpose, sifts through many possibilities, and retains those pursuits that promise to advance that purpose."[13]

An assumption made earlier in this essay was that the individual is personally responsible for continuing education. As Rouch reminds the minister, "You are the dean of your own continuing education."[14]

In order for an individual to serve as one's own "dean of continuing education," a clearly understood and functional planning model is needed. The following model is suggested as a guide for planning:

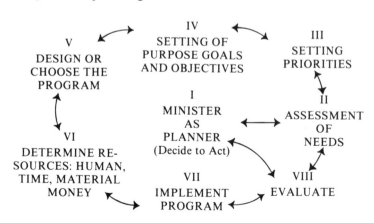

Continuing Education

This model is not intended to be understood as a series of eight carefully orchestrated steps that one slavishly follows. Rather, this is a planning *system*. That is, each subsystem of the system is linked with each of the other subsystems. Information generated at each point within the system further informs the entire system. Here is how each subsystem might work:

I. Minister as Planner

The motivation for involvement and decision to act would come at this point. The minister assumes responsibility for initiating the process.

II. Assessment of Needs

The minister begins to ask such personal and probing questions as these: What are my strengths or weaknesses? What is required for me to be the minister God is calling me to be? Of the forty-six competencies, which ones do I need to improve?

Perhaps several assessment instruments will be used. Guidance from trusted colleagues could be helpful. Feedback from the laity could give a clearer focus on particular needs.

III. Setting Priorities

Setting priorities is very important. Although the needs that surface during the assessment phase might be many and varied, not all of these can be dealt with immediately. Sorting out and choosing from alternatives will enable the minister to identify those areas of concern that need attention now. Other concerns are held in reserve until further opportunities become available.

IV. Setting of Purposes, Goals, Objectives

It might be helpful to understand each of these three terms as they are being used here:

Purpose answers the *why* question. Why does one become involved in continuing education? The minister thinks seriously about reasons and begins to list these as a way to develop a clear rationale for time, energy, and financial commitment. For example, one purpose statement might be this: I am involved in continuing education to become a more effective communicator of the Word of God.

Goals point to *what* one values as an end result. Goals are broad and overarching. They give the target toward which to direct resources. A goal that would relate to purpose previously stated might be this: I am involved in continuing education to increase my skills in preaching.

Objectives are specific and point to *how* one goes about reaching a goal. Following through on the preceding examples, an objective might be this: I plan to attend one preaching clinic during this year.

V. Design or Choose Program

Having assessed needs, determined priorities, and developed purposes, goals, and objectives, the minister is ready either to design an individual program or choose from the many existing programs. Phase VI as well as preceding phases will no doubt need to inform the design and choice processes.

VI. Determine Resources

What resources are available to the minister? Being aware of a variety of settings and opportunities is crucial. More information on resources will be given later. Suffice it here to suggest that the minister needs to ask about time commitments, financial resources, facilities or equipment needed, human resources available, and similar matters.

Continuing Education

VII. Implement the Program

The time has now come to begin to do what has been carefully planned. The program is available, the resources are allocated, and the minister is involved in one or more significant growth experiences.

VIII. Evaluation

How well is the plan working? Is the continuing-education plan helping to achieve the stated purposes, reach the stated goals, and fulfill the objectives? If not, why? Where does the minister go from here? What is the next step?

Perhaps the planning model as described appears a bit cumbersome and involved. That could be because planning is not typically a high priority for ministers. Or it could be that the model is new and not yet understood. Or (alas) it could be because the model *is* cumbersome and involved. Perhaps a better or simpler model could be followed.

Whatever the case, planning one's continuing-education program is crucial. The importance of planning is illustrated well in the following parable:

Parable of the Sea Horse

Once upon a time a Sea Horse gathered up his seven pieces of eight and cantered out to find his fortune. Before he had traveled far he met an Eel, who said, "Psst! Hey, bud. Where 'ya going?"

"I'm going out to find my fortune," replied the Sea Horse proudly.

"You're in luck," said the Eel. "For four pieces of eight you can have this speedy flipper, and then you'll be able to get there a lot faster."

"Gee, that's swell," said the Sea Horse, and paid the money and put on the flipper and slithered off at twice the speed.

Soon he came upon a Sponge, who said, "Psst! Hey bud. Where 'ya going?"

"I'm going out to find my fortune," replied the Sea Horse.

"You're in luck," said the Sponge. "For a small fee I will let you have this jet-propelled scooter so that you will be able to travel a lot faster."

So the Sea Horse bought the scooter with his remaining money and went zooming thru the sea five times as fast. Soon he came upon a Shark, who said, "Psst! Hey bud. Where 'ya going?"

"I'm going out to find my fortune," replied the Sea Horse.

"You're in luck. If you'll take this short cut," said the Shark, pointing to his open mouth, "you'll save yourself a lot of time."

"Gee, thanks," said the Sea Horse, and zoomed off into the interior of the Shark, there to be devoured.

The moral of this fable is that if you're not sure where you're going, you're liable to end up someplace else.[15]

METHODS AND SETTINGS FOR CONTINUING EDUCATION

When considering a continuing-education plan, the minister needs to be aware of at least two concerns. First, what methods are valued most? Second, what are some settings for continuing education?

Methods

One exciting thing about continuing education is that it is not bound to one method in a structured classroom setting. Methods can vary with the needs and interests of the person and with the content to be learned. Here is a short sampling of approaches that are used in continuing education:

1. Lecture: Involves a structured presentation by a recognized authority. A variety of lectureships are offered for the enrichment of clergy.

Continuing Education

2. Discussion: Led by a person who brings expertise in both subject matter and skills in discussion leadership.

3. Reading: Carefully chosen books, journals, and the like that when read critically and reflectively, enhance personal growth in ministry.

4. Media Resources: A variety of media resources are available including printed curriculum, film, tapes (audio and video), television, telephone hook-ups, and radio.

5. Workshops/ Clinics: A method in which skills are learned and practiced under careful supervision and evaluation.

6. Observation/ Travel: Includes museums, art galleries, government or religious assemblies, transcultural experiences, travel abroad.

7. Colleague Clusters: Intensive involvement in a group over a stated period of time for personal growth and learning.

8. Research: Systematic inquiry in a concentrated area of concern, resulting in new knowledge and understanding for the researcher.

Settings

Methods do vary in continuing education. In order to accommodate a variety of methodologies, numerous settings are utilized for study. The following are merely representative of the many settings in which continuing education might take place:

1. Home: Individual, self-directed study utilizing prepared home study curriculum or personal library resources.

2. Minister's Study: A workshop and retreat setting sanctified for personal prayer, meditation,

study, reflection, and preparation.

3. Public Facilities: Library, museum, art gallery, and the like where reading, observation, or research can take place.

4. Church Facilities: Conferences, seminars, workshops, colleague clusters that are served best by being in a church facility.

5. Local Institutions: Hospitals, mental health centers, prisons, and the like in which clinical opportunities are available.

6. Universities and Colleges: Opportunities for training in a variety of subjects and interest areas; often financially underwritten for clergy.

7. Seminaries: For alumni, denominational ministers, transdenominational experiences of short term or long term duration for credit toward a degree or noncredit CEU.

8. Denominational Agencies: State, regional, or national agencies in a variety of settings; concerns such as education, missions, and ministry.

9. Conference Centers: A variety of events are sponsored usually with excellent leadership.

Other methods and settings for continuing education can be added to the previous two listings. These are illustrative of the fact that the minister who is serious about continuing education can find ways and settings in which he or she can be involved. There is no dearth of opportunity.

THE CHURCH AND CONTINUING EDUCATION FOR MINISTRY

The focus of this essay has been expressly upon continuing education of the clergy. Some basic assumptions are inherent in such a focus.

Continuing Education

First, our is a rapidly changing world. Continuing education for clergy is parallel to continuing education in other fields such as medicine, law, business, farming, and auto mechanics to name a few. Lay persons in such fields are quite aware of the need to keep abreast of new knowledge and skills.

Second, the Church is concerned about the growth of persons in ministry. The laity must support the minister in planning a continuing-education program. Emotional support, financial support, and significant allotment of time are all necessary to a well-rounded continuing-education program.

Third, growth in competency for ministry will result in corresponding creative change with the Church. Continuing education for ministers is not seen as a private, individualistic experience. Rather, it is seen in the context of the entire community of believers whom the minister serves.

This third assumption needs more attention. If clergy growth is to result in creative congregational change, the laity must be involved at strategic points in the continuing-education process. The argument might be made that specific clergy concerns need to be isolated and dealt with by clergy groups only. Such concerns are likely few in number.

Another perspective would view ministry as the calling of all the people of God. Ministry is the mutual task of clergy and laity. Many of the forty-six competencies for ministry listed earlier are competencies also needed by the laity for effectiveness in their ministries. Laity and clergy can learn and grow together with effective results.

Whenever creative organizational change is a value, learning of clergy and laity together becomes increasingly more important. Clergy often go alone to a training event with the intention of returning to implement some new creative program. Research has shown that such individualistic efforts do produce individual growth but only about 13 percent effectiveness in applying what was learned in the back-home situation. Whenever laity accompany clergy to training events, the back-home application of knowledge and skills increases substantially.[16]

Another important consideration is the increasing distancing of clergy from the laity. A number of years ago Hadden observed that a wide gulf was developing between clergy and laity.[17] Such a gulf is likely the product of such things as language differences, conceptual barriers, and differing role expectations.

If mutual and cooperative ministry is to occur in the Church, this gulf will need to be closed. One way to work at this concern is to involve laity and clergy together in significant learning opportunities!

THE FUTURE OF CONTINUING EDUCATION IN MINISTRY

A growing church requires a growing minister. The United Presbyterian church was losing members. A research project was conducted to determine the reasons for the loss. A variety of reasons was discovered. However, one unanticipated piece of information resulted from the study. A number of Presbyterian churches were growing. The researchers sought to find out the key to their growth. The study indicated that in each case the growing churches had vital pastoral leadership showing competency in preaching, pastoral calling, communicating warmth and sensitivity to members, and an ability to generate enthusiasm and spiritual authenticity.[18]

The future of continuing education is crucial to ministry. It is not only a hedge against boredom for the clergy, but also a key to effective church growth.

With this affirmation firmly stated, this essay concludes with the following vision for continuing education in the decades ahead:

1. Continuing education will become a concern of the total church.
2. The seminary will be only one of several agencies and

institutions that have important contributions to make to the planning, staffing, and financing of continuing education.

3. Continuing education of ministers will not take place in a vacuum, but will be planned and carried out in closer relationship with the laity so that the ministry of the whole church will be enriched.

4. Continuing education will be appropriate and accessible to all practicing clergy regardless of their educational status or limitations of previous training.

5. Specific programs of continuing education will be planned and made available to persons who serve in unique situations and cultural settings.

6. Serious research will be conducted on area, regional, and national levels to determine needs and resources for continuing education for ministry.

Notes

1. For a discussion of the variety of ways clergy are living out their ministry see Carnegie Samuel Calian, *Today's Pastor in Tomorrow's World* (Philadelphia: The Westminster Press, 1982). 15-40.

2. Robert K. Greenleaf has treated this biblical model most thoroughly in his book *Servant Leadership: A Journey into the Nature of Legitimate Power and Greatness* (Ramsey, N.J.: Paulist Press, 1977).

3. The ministry is not the only profession experiencing burnout. For a helpful discussion of professional burnout see Jerry Edelwich with Archie Brodsky, *Burn-Out: Stages of Disillusionment in the Helping Professions* (New York: Human Sciences Press, 1980).

4. Mark Rouch, *Competent Ministry: A Guide to Effective Continuing Education* (Nashville: Abingdon Press, 1974), 16-17.

5. The United Methodist church has recently placed a continuing-education requirement upon its clergy. Congregational finan-

cial support is a part of the package. The progress of such a mandate will be interesting to follow.

6. Margaret Mead, "A Redefinition of Education," *Journal of the NEA* 48 (October 1959), 15-17.

7. For insight into this question, the following sources would be quite helpful: James D. Glasse, *Profession: Minister* (Nashville: Abingdon Press, 1968); Urban T. Holmes, III, *The Future Shape of Ministry* (New York: The Seabury Press, 1971); Henri J. Nouwen, *Creative Ministry* (New York: Doubleday & Co., 1971); Donald P. Smith, *Clergy in the Cross Fire* (Philadelphia: The Westminster Press, 1973).

8. Nathan M. Pusey, *Ministry for Tomorrow: Report of the Special Committee on Theological Education* (New York: The Seabury Press, 1967), 45-51.

9. Henri J. Nouwen, *The Wounded Healer* (New York: Doubleday & Co., 1972).

10. Calian, *Today's Pastor*, p. 124ff.

11. Boards of Ministry and Theological Schools have been tireless in attempts to establish competencies for ministry. One of the most thorough attempts in recent years is the "Readiness for Ministry" project sponsored by the Association of Theological Schools. Their report is in David S. Schuller, Milo L. Brekke, and Merton P. Strommen, eds., *Readiness For Ministry*, vol. 1, *Criteria* (The Association of Theological Schools in the United States and Canada, 1975). Also see Steve Clapp, *Ministerial Competency Report* (Sidell, Illinois: C-4 Resources, 1982).

12. See Rouch, *Competent Ministry*, pp. 100-139.

13. Connolly C. Gamble, Jr., "The Continuing Education of Ministers," *Proceeding, 1966 Navy Supervisory Chaplains Conference* (Washington, D.C.: Bureau of Navy Personnel: Chaplains Division, 1966), 226.

14. Rouch, *Competent Ministry*, p. 49.

15. Robert Mager, *Preparing Instructional Objectives* (Palo Alto, Calif.: Fearon Publishers, 1962), ix.

Continuing Education

16. For a discussion of the values in clergy-layperson training together see Paul M. Dietterich, *Clergy Growth and Church Vitalization* (Naperville, Ill.: The Center for Parish Development, 1979), 23-60.

17. Jeffrey Hadden, *The Gathering Storm in the Churches* (New York: Doubleday & Co., 1969).

18. Calian, *Today's Pastor,* 19-20.

Jerry C. Grubbs

Tomorrow and Thereafter
Louis Paul Meyer

Obedience to Christ today is demanding that the Church and each Christian become better students of the future. Every person and family, institution, and nation is affected by the future and in turn has an effect on the future. Some feel the future is *fixed* and that human beings cannot change it. Others feel God gave to human beings the capacity and freedom to make choices that affect and help to shape the future. People of hope with a vision can make a very significant difference.

The idea of the future is one of the central symbols through which human beings have ordered their present lives and given meaning to their past. Concern and fascination with the future is as old as the human race. Our most distant ancestors were as concerned about the blessings, tragedies, and accidents that would shape their lives as we are today. People of old consulted oracles, soothsayers, shamans, fortunetellers, prophets, and even the stars in an attempt to peer into the future and prepare for it. But the way people see the future and the tools they use to influence it have changed dramatically through the ages. Future planning and predictions of the future now absorb a considerable portion of the energies invested in our major institutions. Industrial, governmental, and academic organizations are committed to long-range forecasting and future exploration for the sake of their own development and that of the society. The Church is challenged to become a better student of the future. Church leaders are beginning to devote more time and energies to research and planning for the future.

We are living in a time in which past forms of life and ways of thinking are disappearing. New forms are arising. A new vision of reality is beginning to emerge. For the future, our adjustment is not to some permanent condition of life, but to the process of continuous change. Constant change is the widespread reality of our time. Our adjustment to this fact in the universe is basically an adjustment within the human intelligence. This adjustment requires us to change our perspective of life.

Ours is a time in which we move from one phase of development to another, from one problem to another, rather than from solution to solution. The whole human family faces the *same* future. Some key concepts for the decade ahead include interdependence, interrelatedness, wholeness, oneness, and joint survival. An overarching issue is human and planetary survival.

All living things are in serious trouble throughout our planet. Food shortages, pollution of our water, earth, and air, massive human starvation, and the disappearance of many species of animal and plant life are grim evidences that we are now endangering our entire planetary system. This raises serious issues and questions for the Church. Our Christian response will be shaped by these issues.

GLOBAL ISSUES

Every citizen on spaceship earth is familiar with the many serious problems that human beings, technology, and progress-at-any-cost methods have brought upon the earth. Each of us doubtless has a personal list of abuses.

We must awaken again to the realities and wonders of the earth! This is basic for a meaningful survival and future. The entire human venture depends on a quality of awe, reverence, and joy in the earth, including all that lives and grows upon the earth. For we, too, are among these living things.

Humanity has forgotten that the earth is a manifestation of divine power and spiritual presence. The predominant and paralyzing view today sees earth merely as a deposit of natural resources, placed here for humanity's wanton use.

Thankfully for earth's creatures, many biologists, physicists, conservationists, and ecologists are beginning to get the attention of some of the rest of us, pointing out the horror inherent in this type of attitude.[1]

The land is central to life on this planet. This was a fact well understood by the native American. It is the only planet we have, but in the past two centuries it has been treated as a mere thing placed here for destruction by human beings. With the unprecedented growth in world population, coupled with our reckless use of resources, evidence is mounting daily that some nonrenewable resources are being used up at an alarming rate. The list includes aluminum, copper, gold, tin, mercury, lead, and oil.

An intensive study was conducted by thirty individuals from ten countries, including scientists, educators, economists, industrialists, and international civil servants. They concluded that if the present growth trends in world population, industrialization, pollution, food production, and resource depletion continue unchanged, the limits to growth for this planet will be reached within the next one hundred years.[2] The most probable result will be a rather sudden and uncontrollable decline in both population and industrial capacity.

They also conclude that these growth trends can be altered and a condition of ecological and economic stability established that is sustainable far into the future. This state of global equilibrium must be designed so that the basic material needs of each person on earth be satisfied and each person has an equal opportunity to realize her or his individual human potential. If the world's people decide to strive for this, the sooner they begin working to attain it, the greater will be their chances of success.

CONSUMPTION

The rate at which the world markets consume materials and nonrenewable resources is growing at an alarming pace. Perhaps the best illustration of this is the world consumption of petroleum. With our insatiable appetite for petroleum, even if all oil companies make more discoveries, we as a world cannot cope if the scale of consumption is not addressed. If the early 1970's rate were continued we would have to find the equivalent of a new Saudi Arabian oil field every three years just to keep up with growing consumption. Leveling out periods of oil consumption are anticipated, but the predictions are that the pace will quicken again before the end of this decade.

What are our options? Some suggest that we should freeze the consumption at the present level. But to do so means that the underdeveloped nations would be grossly without the sufficient energy needed for their livelihood and development. Another possible solution would be for Western and developed nations to share with the underdeveloped nations in some type of redistribution of the resources and wealth. This would require a drastic change in life-style for individuals and nations. No evidence presently exists that any nation is giving serious consideration to this alternative.

A related critical issue will come more sharply into focus in this decade. The Western nations in general and the United States in particular, consume far more than their fair share of the earth's resources. According to United Nations population data, persons in America comprise approximately 6 percent of the world's population. Nevertheless, this 6 percent consumes over 30 percent of the world's petroleum, approximately 42 percent of the world's total output of aluminum, and 44 percent of the world's output of coal.

INFLATION AND ENERGY

The worldwide phenomenon of inflation has created numerous types of problems and has raised issues for the world's people. According to most projections, this cancerous economic condition will continue on a worldwide scale throughout the eighties.

Scarcity is an absolute fact of life. Regardless of what we read or hear, sufficient energy is not available at the present rate of consumption and with the present rate of population growth to bring the world up to the Western standard of living. We built a dream of abundance in the 1950s and 1960s, but that dream was short lived. During that time we also had the dream that technology would overcome scarcity, but that too was only an illusion.

In the 1950s the prevailing view was that the rest of the world, the so-called Third World, should be developed as the Western nations were developed. Aid was given and hopes were raised for India, Latin America, Africa, and other nations. But in the 1960s some world shortages began to become apparent. The realization became increasingly evident that these nations with vast populations could not be developed using the Western nations as the norm.

Sufficient energy and materials are simply not available. Also, the destructive nature of technology used to develop the Western countries is intolerable. The West has set a pattern of life that cannot and should not be universalized.

FOOD AND WATER

Food and water are global issues. Both have become more pronounced social issues as the decade of the 1980s unfolds. In the United States as well as in the rest of the world, food production, distribution, and consumption will be key issues.

Today OPEC and petroleum are in the world spotlight. As the 1980s pass, the prediction has been set forth that the United States and our production of food will be in the spotlight. With our rich land, adequate rains, and favorable weather, we as a nation are in the position of producing far more food than we need. How will we use it? To whom will we sell it? At what price?

The next crisis to hit North America and the world will be water shortages. We tend to forget that the same water we drink today quenched the thirst of the dinosaurs. It is recycled again and again through sunshine, evaporation, formation of clouds, and rain returning to the ocean with the cycle repeating itself again and again. Water is not manufactured.

The quantity has been the same since the creation of time. If not hopelessly interrupted by human ignorance and greed, nature has a marvelous ability to take the water that has gone through muddy streams, sewage systems, dishwashers, and garbage disposals and purify it again and again. But nature's way takes a long time. Technology can do it faster, but it is much more expensive and not cost effective. A much more judicial use of water must be devised.

LAND CONTROL

More and more of the world's land is in the control of fewer and fewer people. Conglomerate energy corporations are expanding their control over mineral-rich land. For example, many oil companies have taken over coal and mineral lands in the United States. Seven corporations own 32 percent of the private lands in the state of Maine. Absentee landlords own or control two-thirds of the private land in West Virginia. Such ownership is a growing trend throughout the world. This issue will come into sharper focus relative to fairness, justice, and the best land use for human good.

Ready or not, like it or not, the United States is completely tied to the rest of the world. Every issue listed previously is a priority concern to the United States. One perspective that is new for Americans as well as citizens of other nations is that we are *global citizens.*

The Vietnam War has undermined every aspect of our national American life. Our belief in our invincible power as a nation, our trust that our government always tells us the truth, and our estimate of our private level of morality have all been undermined by that war. The TV image of middle-class American gentility has been unmasked by the war, crime at home, bombings, bizarre plane hijackings, kidnappings, and shocking assassinations.

These events have brought about vast attitudinal changes in Americans about themselves and their nation. A loss of assurance has occurred concerning America's course of social progress. The American people's faith in social progress, government programs, and human rationality has been greatly shaken. This could result in some irrational action in the unpredictable eighties.

CONSUMERISM

After World War II, the great American industrial machine that had tooled up to repel the aggression of Japan and Germany had a tremendous capacity for continued production. After peace, the question of product distribution arose with all the technological know-how we had gained through the war experience. Madison Avenue provided the answer to this production distribution question: Advertise to convince the purchasing public that it should buy everything our factories could produce. If they already had the basics— food, clothing, and shelter—and many of them had the depression mentality, how could you convince them to buy? Again, the answer was simple: "Because it is *new!*" For the past thirty-five years, whatever is new is somehow subtly identified with the good. This has brought about a change not only in our habits of consumption, but also in our total philosophy and outlook on life.

A good illustration of this is the Barbie doll. In 1959 the Mattel Toy Company introduced the Barbie doll to little girls of America. Since then, ninety-eight million dolls have been sold. Later Mattel announced that they were coming out with a *new* model. This new, improved Barbie doll had a slimmer figure, real eyelashes, and a twist-turn waist. To provide more incentive to purchase they announced that the old Barbie doll could be used as a trade-in on the new one! Little girls gladly turned in their old Barbie dolls for new models. As children, their mothers and grandmothers had clutched lingeringly and lovingly to the same dolls until the cherished playthings disintegrated from age.

This incessant demand for the new builds obsolescence directly into the marketplace so that there is no end to the demand. Consumptive lust will not allow us to be spiritually free from material things.

POPULATION TRENDS

According to the 1980 census, people age sixty-five and over will account for one of every eight U.S. citizens by 1990.[3] Thirty million such Americans will be in this category by then. Twelve million of them will be seventy-five years and over. Blacks will increase in proportion to whites, and will make up approximately 12.2 percent of the population. Hispanics will increase to approximately the same population size as blacks, and Asians will double their percentage of the population, totaling in excess of three million. Approximately twenty million new additions will be made to the population in the decade of the eighties, bringing the U.S. total to approximately 242 million by 1990. The number of Americans under twenty years of age will fall below 30 percent of the total population for the first time in our nation's history. Fifty percent of women twenty-four to fifty-four years of age worked or sought paid jobs in 1970; 70 percent of the same age group of women will be in the job market by 1990. This is a total of thirty-eight million women.

Ministry Tomorrow and Thereafter

The church is not ministering adequately to the vast majority of the U.S. population. This vast majority includes single-parent families, divorced persons, and the never married. These and other persons do not fit the American family stereotype—of a young husband and wife with children under eighteen. Such families actually make up only 34 percent of the population.[4]

A key social and religious issue of the eighties will be *ethnicity*. Within church circles, the issue of ethnicity will be affected by the degree to which the dominant whites within church groups allow the ethnic groups associated in their fellowship to establish viable and strong identities apart from the dominant white traditions. This will heighten the need of the newcomer to go beyond equality to assess the meaning of her or his background and personal heritage.

As each ethnic group strives for its own uniqueness, at the same time trying to be a part of the whole of American society, extra understanding and assistance as well as freedom for development must be allowed by the majority. Competitive tension for jobs, goods, houses, and creative living will increase with the rise of inflation. This always tends to heighten differences and clashes between majority and minority. Often in such times the majority allows or encourages differences between minorities.

ASPIRATIONS

In this decade let us recognize that in spite of the vast scientific achievements of the past and regardless of the incalculable potential of our technology, we are not going to save ourselves from our present dilemma with a quick technological fix. Our problems are too deep and complex for that. Even Herman Kahn, the futurist who had done much to further the cause of technology, says the problems that must be faced for the rest of this century are more theological than technological, and the next twenty-five years ought to be given to the question of the meaning and purpose of life rather than to some new form of technology.[5]

This has tremendous implications for the Church and Education.

We are going to have to learn to make some choices and establish a world system of values for making decisions and trade-offs. For example, we cannot have inexpensive industrial processing and an unpolluted ecosphere. We must trade off one or the other. In order to guarantee the availability of nonrenewable natural resources in the future, policies must be adopted now that will decrease resources use in the present. In a day of limited resources, do we want more food for the poor or more services for the rich? Ultimate survival or self-annihilation? Careless taking of nature's resources or concern for tomorrow's ecological balance? Gluttonous self-indulgence or sharing of our good production with the poor and hungry?

Somehow we must aspire to recognize that all people of the world are participants in a common universal drama. Our world is a *single* planetary society for good or ill. Through TV and modern communication, both we and our children are citizens of the global village.

THE CHURCH FOR THE FUTURE

The Church is the body of believers called to be God's servant people. Christianity is a religion for tough times. The future is always unknown. The signs of our times suggest high risks and potentially the nuclear annihilation of our world. But from a Christian perspective we also see woven through this future a tough thread of faith and hope that in times of trouble and crisis will not break. Instead, these times can transform defeats into victories. God is the God not only of Abraham, Isaac, and Jacob, but also of the future. He is out ahead of us calling the Church to be his servant people, beckoning the Church to be the people of faith helping others in this confused world to get a new vision and become truly the people of God. *In these times of uncertainty, God wants the Church to be questioners of accepted assumptions and clarifiers of options available to humankind.* The congregation, church movement, or individual Christian that has caught Jesus' vision of the new day, the new wineskin, the new cloth, and the new spirit will be best able to represent Christ in this decade and the next.

The church of the future must deal with all these tasks:

1. Help society get a larger perspective, beyond self, family, city, state, and nation, and view the future from a *global perspective.*
2. Develop a holistic vision of all creation. The human being is a combination of mind, body, soul, and spirit. Human beings need one another and are dependent on one another. Also, human life depends upon an earth that is the source of our health and well-being.
3. Develop a new vision of the earth and universe. Go back to the biblical images of the kingdom of God and develop new meanings of this for today's world. A vision is needed that will inspire people to bury their differences and move on to the task of achieving the world God intends.
4. Demonstrate by its example a more responsible Christian life-style. In the coming era of limits, the Church can make a difference in bringing about better equity for all people by developing and living by a theology of enough.
5. Be more prophetic in its life, work, and deeds. The future will require the Church to call persons, institutions, and the nation to accountability in areas of justice, help for the poor and hungry, disarmament, and peace building. We are on the brink of a vast new conquest of the oceans and outer space. Will the resources in these two vast areas be developed justly and peacefully?
6. Set a better example of the stewardship of life and of all earth's resources. All of life—human, animal, and earth —is sacred and belongs to God. How much growth in population and consumption of natural resources can the planet stand?
7. Affirm pluralism and variety as the plan of God. God's

world includes many species of plants, trees, flowers, animals, and fish. He also created people with a wide variety of cultures, customs, and gifts. The church of the future must find ways to affirm this and help others accept it as God's plan.

8. Help the world see that the future world is being created by what we do now! The future is not being imposed as some mysterious external force. It does not just happen to us; we ourselves create it by what we do or fail to do. With a new vision of the future, the Church can help the world focus more on what we want the future to be. The world of tomorrow will arise from the cumulative acts of several billion everyday people who feel they have no influence whatsoever. Yet, these everyday people are the real shapers of history.

9. Relate faith to the future. We must be realistic about the uncertainty of the times, but always tempered with hope based on faith in God and his control of the future.

10. Respond from the perspective of biblical faith and heritage, rather than economic and culturally based perspective. The Church is in a strategic position today to help shape the future through a biblical view of the future, which includes a life of assurance, faith, hope and a world in which peace is not only possible, but attainable.

Notes

1. Examples of this can be found in such writings as the following:

　　A. Harold Schilling, *The New Consciousness in Science and Religion* (Philadelphia: Pilgrim Press, 1972). A physicist writing in lay terms from a Christian perspective.

　　B. Rene' Dubois, *The God Within* (New York: Charles Scribner's Sons, 1972).

　　C. Paul Lutz and Paul Santimire, *Ecological Renewal* (Philadelphia: Fortress Press, 1972).

Ministry Tomorrow and Thereafter

2. O. L. and D. H. Meadows, *The Limits to Growth: A Report from the Club of Rome's Project on the Predicament of Mankind* (New York: Universe Books, 1972).

3. 1980 Census of Population.

4. The Parish Paper, 1980 Series, by Lyle Schaller, Yokefellow Institute, Richmond, Indiana.

Herman Kahn in a speech delivered at the First Global Conference on the Future, July 20-24, 1980, Toronto, Canada.